Negative Capitalism

Cynicism in the Neoliberal Era

Negative Capitalism

Cynicism in the Neoliberal Era

J. D. Taylor

Winchester, UK
Washington, USA

First published by Zero Books, 2013
Zero Books is an imprint of John Hunt Publishing Ltd., Laurel House, Station Approach,
Alresford, Hants, SO24 9JH, UK
office1@jhpbooks.net
www.johnhuntpublishing.com
www.zero-books.net

For distributor details and how to order please visit the 'Ordering' section on our website.

Text copyright: J. D. Taylor 2012

ISBN: 978 1 78099 260 0

A CIP catalogue record for this book is available from the British Library.

Design: Stuart Davies

Printed and bound by CPI Group (UK) Ltd, Croydon, CR0 4YY

We operate a distinctive and ethical publishing philosophy in all
areas of our business, from our global network of authors to
production and worldwide distribution.

CONTENTS

The Argument

Each of us lives in an era where our social lives are determined by financial capital. The scale of debts owed collectively to invisible and unknown creditors is the pretext for increased demands for productivity and consumption, in exchange for vastly increasing living costs, rents, and reductions in social securities and real wages. Each of us has little agency or control over these circumstances, whilst distant banks and an aloof and privately-educated political class intensify their control and management over our everyday lives. Everything (and everyone) begins to break down under the pressure of being a productive consumer, anger and dissent are internalised, self-inflicted, erupting momentarily, whilst a discredited neoliberal political ideology and caste of financial capitalists increase their privateering enclosure of public wealth by the day. This is an era of negative capitalism, where one's individual and collective capabilities and quality of life are steadily diminished and disempowered by financial capital. This negation of individuals into economically productive behaviours represents, in the second decade of the 21st century, a new kind of era, with specific disorders (depression, anxiety), specific devices (the internet, smart-phone, and laptop) and a new cultural feeling (cynicism).

The argument here is that many singular discontents with financial capitalism can be understand within a wider process of negation, a process of disempowerment embedded in financial capitalism and primarily transmitted through a corruption of language, and hence thought. To explain this new framework, I'll outline what neoliberalism is in theory and practice, what I mean by negative capitalism, and how this analysis fits into existing accounts of capitalism, before using the bulk of the work to explore specific symptoms of negativity and the peculiar cynicism of the contemporary era. There is no "we" here. No "should"s or "would"s. I won't insult the reader's intelligence by claiming that there's a coming change on the horizon, if everyone waits a little longer, or that there's a magical solution here that's never been considered before, a cipher that when uttered transforms everything irredeemably anew. I am 24 years old, a worker and 'a graduate without a future', and I do not write from a position of academic, social or political privilege: my only stake in financial capitalism is a five figure debt. I am profoundly angry and depressed by what I see around me, but I am also hopeful that a new era can be created by this generation, provided the blurry errors of history, cynicism and individualism can be traded in for strategy and a new social democracy, underlined by a revolution of citizens in law and constitution.

This work differs from other recent analyses, which have often focused on one singular aspect of late capitalism, by offering an overarching framework for understanding the problems of the contemporary era in terms of 'negation' – a collective disempowerment of the public by financial capitalism. It goes ahead and describes specific strategies to challenge negative capitalism and create a counter-politic of social democracy. I make this kind of incautious and bold analysis in order to foment public debate regarding strategy. There is an abundance of nuanced and theoretically subtle arguments that fail to engage an enraged socially-democratic public on its own terms. Therefore this work aims to challenge both the informed reader and the new reader of political philosophy. The work aims to detail the scale of the problem: negative capitalism and its existential costs, and the cultural effects of cynicism. Rather than reel off just a utopian fairy-world of *what* and *why*, the intention here is to focus additionally on *how*, on strategy. I do not claim to know how exactly we all should live, or that 'we all' (assuming that all of you already agree with me, another conceit to avoid) should act or behave in one way or another. The aim is to stimulate response with a series of wild, occasionally arrogant and deliberately

2

inflammatory arguments. The argument does offer a solution to the problems of negative capitalism – what is described here as social democracy – but this concept is offered to provoke discussion above all else. Cynical passivity is the problem. Nothing less than a basic quality of life is the prize and the end.

I

What is Negative Capitalism?

When was the last time you had a couple of days of just relaxation, without the pretext of a holiday, which didn't involve checking emails, buying things, or guiltily trying to catch up with undernourished relationships? When did you last get through a month without having to borrow even more money so that you could actually eat, meet your rent payment and afford public transport? Can you recall the last Monday or Tuesday you got through where you didn't at one point experience a feeling of fairly moderate terror and anxiety during the daily email bombardment? In an era of negative capitalism, life itself becomes negated and alienated from its sources of happiness and social support. Relaxation is accompanied by guilt. Debt becomes a social and political condition.

Since 2010 the political terrain of the UK has irreversibly shifted, hence the necessity of writing about these problems now under a wider conceptual framework of negation. Anger against the capitalist Real has erupted with small but symbolically powerful successes. Many working-class and 'underclass' young people in British urban areas have demonstrated that they feel they have no stake in their communities, demonstrated in the violence inflicted on their own alienated communities and on colonising chainstores during the August 2011 riots. Meanwhile young middle-class graduates have been similarly disinherited by the lack of any real forms of sustainable employment in the country, with similarly abortive strikes of anger against police, parliament and university authorities in a continued wave of local and national actions since 2010. In the second decade of the 21st century, pain, depression and rage in urban communities is tangible. Yet the neoliberal project of privatising public wealth has accelerated to include healthcare, education and the police-force, leaving perhaps only the armed forces and judiciary acting only in the apparent interests of the 'public'. So why hasn't all this deprivation, cuts and growing inequality, in the face of an increasingly arrogant financial culture in the City, not led to a violent overthrow of the political class, or even any nascent organised oppositional movement?

Back in 2009, Mark Fisher persuasively argued in *Capitalist Realism* that the Left needed to overturn popular consent to Capital via a Spinozean return to setting out and determining, in a firm paternalistic manner, the general will of the public. It required the creation of a strange new being straight out of the blog of a postgraduate doleite or a worker's depressive convalescence, a Marxist Supernanny:

> The Marxist Supernanny would not only be the one who laid down limitations, who acted in our own interests when we are incapable of recognizing them ourselves, but also the one prepared to take this kind of risk, to wager on the strange and our appetite for it.[1]

The flattening of desire into a passive anhedonia and the loss of political agency into reflexive impotence could be overturned through a return to the state, subordinating it to the 'general wall' of the public. Back then, the credit crisis had discredited neoliberalism as a model though not defeated it: vast amounts of public money had entered private hands, the collapse of financial capital 'unthinkable'. Fisher's powerful argument back then was that the Left could only compete with Capital by offering an optimistic counter-narrative, one that abandoned the 'ideological rubble' of history with clear promises of reduced bureaucracy and worker autonomy.

In 2012 and 2013, the burden of neoliberalism's costs is clearer – living costs have markedly increased in the last five years, and with that levels of unemployment, homelessness, poverty, and dissatisfaction. The existing functions of the state are increasingly redundant : examples such as the 2009 MPs Parliamentary Expenses Scandal, or the 2011 News International phone-hacking scandal, or the as-yet publicly withheld Motorman files, all reveal the routine lawbreaking, corruption and collusion of elected politicians, police, media proprietors and news editors; whilst key functions of civil society like healthcare, education, housing and policing are becoming privatised and irreversibly damaged by an ineffective and hostile 'Big Society' model. Fisher repeatedly targets Capital itself, but this gives a disparate series of institutions, buildings, individuals and duplicitous agreements an intimidating abstract power. Alternatively, the apparatuses of power that oppress people collectively can be grasped within the effects of 'negativity', administered by a network of financial capitalists, influenced by neoliberal theory, and possessed by a charmless psychotic cynicism that speaks only of the individual. To generate strategies that can be localised and graspable, perhaps rather than state-building as a united left, groups might come together, educate and inspire each other, agree targets and demands, highlight and where possible peacefully disrupt the institutions of financial capital – its internet networks, power-sources, transport networks, stock exchanges – with the intention of breaking passive consent and challenging its hegemony. Disobedience excites and inspires citizens to challenge each other's thinking – what are we doing, what do we want? But at present there is no clear prospect of any counter-political response to financial capitalism, which itself represents a new state of defeat or dormancy, depending on one's capacity for strategic optimism.

This is an era of meltdown, apparently; but beyond the liquefaction of the global financial economy, the real alchemy occurs in turning pensions, schools, and contracts into freefloating, individualised nothingness. Negation isn't a new phenomena, but a relation of power. Applying it to capitalism maps a specific relation to our time based around social and existential diminishment, providing a tidemark from which an atavistic and powerful anger might emerge. If this work seems like little more than another familiar left-leaning cultural studies polemic, reiterating all that is already known, then ask yourself, for how much longer can you hold out clutching onto what little you have? Struggles have stumbled into inactivity; today one is surrounded by somnambulist armies of depressed citizenry, one's intelligence and imagination rarely exercised beyond videogames and Facebook; how much longer can you proceed with the sham that you yourself are different, the special case? How can one call oneself a communist or a socialist, even a democrat, yet patently fail then to enact the necessary strategies and actions of these convictions? The delusion of the individual is the last refuge of the negated. When does the superior intelligence of the collectivity realise itself? When is mild indignation sublimated into real atavistic anger?

Scavenging among ruins where nothing is offered to everyone. The future itself as the closing down sale of a burnt-out 99p store, wild investors called Seb and Giles tearing around inside on stolen mobility scooters. Clipped conversations, looped beats, twisted tales of old school mates or London's male suicide rate. Thwarted attempts to leave the capital. Determined to begin again, anew, entirely. On one south London living room wall the words of James Connolly: 'the great appear great to us only because we are on our knees: let us rise'. The black and the gold of well-beat nocturnal streets. Answers emerging on the tip of the lip, etched inside eyelids.

Whilst some of the problems of the contemporary era might not be ended with the demise of the financial institutions, they are the discredited caste of an irrational age, and can be swept away. The credit crisis of 2008 has led to a profound global depression and decline in living standards for the majority of human life, those who did not cause and who have not benefited before or since the manipulation of credit, but whose lives have been effectively colonised by debt, the tribute of future earnings to banking institutions. The progressivism of historical materialism, that humans can collectively act for their good, is easily suspect: our peers are easily manipulated by hot words, persuaded by their bellies as much as the limits of their rational understanding. We are equally dependent and bored by the 'miracle, mystery and authority' that legitimises financial capitalism, as meted out by an regressive cabal of flabby bankers, corrupt politicians and manically-egotistical media owners. Change needs to be determined by charismatic working-class leaders who engage the public, not the academics, with strategic and universal demands that can be protected by new laws and a constitution, militating against the threat of fascism and authoritarianism. If negation is a state of disempowerment of the democracy by a capitalist oligarchy, then power can only be reasserted and retaken by the actions of the democracy and its representatives. It is no easy struggle.

Even though there is no simple solution, there are strategies within grasp that might replace our negative habits acquired under capitalism with new and more organic ones. There is no evidence of a pure or essential natural life that each of us might regain after capitalism; nor is there evidence that human beings will always in every circumstance rationally determine to cooperate peacefully for the 'good': these are two mistaken assumptions socialism has made in the past about human history which are the effects of a monotheistic religious perspective. Neither is human history necessarily 'bad': the point is to understand the nuanced and complex nature of human life, and from this develop strategies for the positive new development of societies by education, democracy, and law. Industrial capitalism has, from its origins in the slavery of cotton plantations and the urban workhouse, been aggressively motivated by the end of private profit and the accumulation of wealth by property-owners, at the expense of workers' lives, health, and natural environments. The private profit motive is intrinsically selfish and destructive of others in its competition. Whilst economically it may seem sustainable, at least to those who succeed and for whom histories are written about, as a social model it injects a violence and aggressive competition into everyday life.

Neoliberalism is the political model of financial capitalism and represents the current political and economic consensus of leaders in Europe, China, and the West. It is an economic argument that unregulated financial trade is the best model for a self-sustaining and meritocratic economy. Whilst it is debatable how fundamentally violent, competitive, or power-seeking human life is, rather than working towards a cooperative and regulated social democracy as I will argue for, declaring capitalism as the best basis for a developed society is danger-ously destructive, crisis-ridden, and ultimately fascistic. Capitalism intrinsically negates individual and collective capacity for equal political representation, social rights, and quality of life, given that its base assumption is that the value of life is determined by its success in individually accumulating and trading wealth. The more powerful capitalism is – that is, the more wealth can be observed to be concentrated in the hands of a very small cabal of effective capitalists – the less the lives of individuals and communities on low-incomes matter. There is no 'good' capitalism, and the system is by no means in a state of crisis, unless perhaps its sustainability is threatened by the growing anger of social democratic revolt across the globe.

Just as there is no positive capitalism, making an old argument for something seemingly opposite like communism is also pretty suspect. Such an idealistic system is very difficult to establish in practice without resorting to totalitarian measures to ensure its own security from war by external capitalist states, worried about unrest in their own impoverished populations.

Instead, a more practical strategy for social transformation is cooperative social democracy, whereby private profit and private property is rendered irrational and illegal, and all things are owned and managed by democratic workers' associations, housing associations, and so on. Social democracy could instead incentivise workers and citizens to develop their workplaces and communities with an appeal to wellbeing, civic responsibility and collective security and happiness. Rather than sulkily waiting for the end of history to level financial capitalism, the opponents of neoliberalism need to start learning from current elites and develop strategies that encourage workers to want to overthrow financial capital. Arguments about its inevitable demise are insufficient. Equal rights and responsibilities need to be legally guaranteed, including access to a living basic wage, shelter, education, healthcare, and employment, being legally-based rights for citizens in a social contract guaranteed by a secular civil constitution. Rights need to be accompanied by responsibilities too, such as the establishment and participation in local and state civil activities and decision-making, observing intelligent compassion and concern for others, and a basic amount of peer-support, training, education, and community work for others in one's locality. These might feel less of a burden in such a social democracy where full employment is guaranteed, meaning that one's hours of productive work would be individually far less than they are currently, where despite the high amount of unemployment, workers are continuously demanded to be more productive in their jobs. Social democracy could celebrate and develop scientific research and cultural activity and production, a key basis of its economy that young people can lead, and could use sustainable and advanced technologies within a Keynesian social framework that pushes tax expenditure into construction and development of infrastructure, local energy production and domestic manufacture, making local areas self-sustaining and therefore more impervious to trade, the archaic basis of the 'middle-man', greed – financial capitalism. In the final case, the aim of social democracy is the creation of an educated and relaxed democratic body, that discuss and vote collectively in their millions for the future of themselves and their communities.

Financial capital introduces an additional sphere of the negative into everyday life. Negativity presents a new means of describing contemporary neoliberal capitalism, a financial being based on control and a fundamental negation of its own presence and time – its *im*materiality, *non*-places, precarity, and time-space compression; the fixed subjectivity and wealth of the nation-state undone by the dark financial algorithms of Capital. Even capitalist time is negated finally as market decisions are made by stock exchange algorithms at preternatural speeds, whilst the market for 'futures' means that experiential time is itself commodified. This negation of time and space has generated a specific kind of anxiety, reflected in increasing anxiety disorders as well as increasing psychological and social breakdowns. Negative capitalism links declining childbirth, relationship instability and malfunctioning families to the increasing demands of total productivity of life by capital. Everything and everyone are plunged into uncertainty, doubt and the inability to grasp essences and an overall sense of things. Its promise of increased speeds and new pleasures comes at the expense of analogue mediums and fixed certainties.

Debt is owed nowhere and to no-one: where exactly is financial capital? Since 1971 there has been no physical grounding for money, and the means in which central banks manage national economies involves less lateral trade and more esoteric mechanisms like recent 'quantitative easing' for instance, where money is created to stimulate economic growth. The unreality of money isn't significant: the way that banks manage an equilibrium of economies through their own purchasing power is more sinister, and despite the continual cycle of crisis in neoliberal capitalism, a far more stable equilibrium has operated, as central banks have acquired greater and greater social resources through state sell-offs of public assets. Financial markets now trade in digits, assets, shares and futures, goods that often do not exist, but on which the fortunes of states, pension-funds, and communities are based. Whilst financial trade may not trade in actual goods, just like the semantically-meaningless language of contemporary politicians examined later, its trade and production of wealth has very real and specific political purposes. Financial capitalism encloses, trades and in its process abstracts publicly-produced wealth into a universal language of financial capital, an abstract code of currency that is privately and competitively traded, motivated by profit and bonuses, which in turn drives capital into a smaller and smaller share of ownership. Its purpose is the maintenance and propagation of itself.

Within the last forty years capitalism has accelerated its extent and permeation of everyday life. Fashion, ideas, and values about the 'self' and beauty, and the techniques and quality of media have been transformed by consumerism, the new social contract of post-World War Two states ("I buy X book, music, clothes, electronic item, therefore I am"). Work in the West has transformed from the factory or family home to the wireless office and internet café, increasingly abstract and knowledge-based with hours of productivity also increasing. Families and relationships break down quicker, workers are more rootless and ready to move to other geographic areas. The public sector has largely been hollowed out and replaced with a part-privatised façade awaiting demolition. There is countless evidence suggesting a more fundamental shift in the social and economic basis of Western societies rather than just simply the passage of a few decades. Locating a specific event that identifies when the neoliberal era began is more difficult.

Was it back in May 1990, when Gilles Deleuze announced that

techniques of power had fundamentally changed, through the collapse of traditional institutions like work, media, and the family, subject to profound changes over the last forty years? Or 15 August 1971, when US president Richard Nixon quit the Bretton Woods agreement and allowed the dollar to become a free-floating financial currency, no longer anchored to the gold standard, marking the beginning of unregulated financial capitalism on a systemic level? If this is too long ago for the contemporary short-circuiting memory, then was it from 1991, when Tim Berners-Lee created hypertext and the world-wide web, that by the end of that decade had already become the most important social medium since TV? Or was it 18 July 2000, with the first broadcast of the UK series of *Big Brother* initiating a new cultural perspective of distorted reality narcissism, popular entertainment provided by CCTV cameras and the apparent zaniness of contestants? *Big Brother* indicated a transformation in the way individuals represented themselves socially, becoming themselves objects and agents of 'reality' media, recording their private intimacies like one's very thoughts or bedroom photography into global digitised information via new internet social networks. Perhaps the change is more recent, say 29 June 2007, with the first release of Apple's iPhone. Again, another social technology that transformed entirely the way the world was represented, listed and engaged with, a new world mediated by lists, logos and memos, a perspective increasingly permeating into everyday working life.

But the transformation to neoliberal capitalism, a negative capitalism, has been a process of political and economic decisions and their implementation over the last forty years, not an event. The cultural and social changes outlined above are all characteristics of the neoliberal era. Life in the UK and US has become gradually negated, compressed, sped-up, and denied. Societies are forced into decline by economic demands for increased productivity, with power abstracted into the digital currency of financial capital, possessed by an invisible government of a financial and political elite. They distort the political process, acquiring media and hence the means of representing societies, and political power through funding and lobbying and hence the means of transforming societies. The basis of managing populations, the art of government, becomes no longer a social but an economic principle.

Living in an era of negative capitalism is far less empowering than any grand summary of the era could suggest. Experiences are intensive, exhausting, continuously connected – boring and anxious in equal measure. Working at any available place or waking hour. Pressure collision, further deprivation necessary: an extra push here, crunch-time there, a freeze in wages. Knowing no-one, being certain of nil. Forced into an ironical and cynical nihilism by political and social shifts over the last forty years that have seen the social contract of modernity shredded, with welfare and a stable wage in exchange for work long gone as financial capitalism and economic production become the sole ideals of a society built on crisis, impervious to collapse through the neatness of its own brutal techniques of power and the vapid homogeneity of its rulers. A vote at the ballot box or attempting to live a meaningful life outside of corrupt and hostile political and economic intervention is a joke, a tawdry fantasy. There is an underground resistance to all this: black humour, casual violence, DIY pornography, alcohol or antidepressant dependency, and above all, cynicism. The primary language of the world has shifted from a religious and imperial language to a financial one. The evidence of negative capitalism is both external and internal, equally measured by the increasing amount of time taken off sick, stressed, or depressed. To feel like nothing: negated, denied, disenfranchised, one's worth assessed by the sum total of data surrounding one's names and appropriate numbers. Without sex, soul, or heart. No longer even labour, work increasingly unpaid or underpaid.

What ever became of you and me, honey? Analytic and text-'heavy' accounts of today's state of play like this are anachronism. Can *Negative Capitalism* be reduced to one screen, to one list, to a set amount of characters? The reduction in attention span is an old lament: Georg Simmel grumbled in 1903 about the blasé metropolitan mindset that by necessity of survival must exclude most sensory impressions to avoid urban neuronal overload. What has changed in the last forty years is the ontological status of the human. A language of citizenship, which connoted being a worker, having values and duties, a certain fixity in status, a stake in political processes by voting and engaging in local government, of having a stake in cultural processes by taking responsibility for one's own personal religious and educational development, and a certain responsibility in social life by actively engaging with local community processes. This has shifted to the status of the consumer, recalled immediately in the language of education, social services and healthcare, where as 'clients' and 'customers' the modern citizen is offered a fundamentally redundant 'choice' that 'empowers' with its 'fairness' to select from a shrinking range of privatised non-options. The modern individual is now a customer, rather than a citizen of the public. The modern citizen is free to borrow from banks and to spend and this is her/his lot and responsibility, the extent of the social contract in contemporary capitalism. It no longer requires a signature or opinion as mark of consent, but a pin code.

The casual alcohol and light drug dependency, occasional self-harm, be it public or private, of one's mid-to-late teens is now traded in for mega-debt levels, being skint and out of time, always a little bit too late. Frenzied working and, in between that, friends rarely seen. The laptop screen is the window through which a continuously awake and alert world bombards our neurones with to-do emails, Viagra spam, narcissism, rolling catastrophes, and DIY porn. This ontological shift in the status of the human is one of the essential reasons for the profound sense of malaise and depression one feels in young adults today. This way of living simply isn't enough, and when one either cannot or chooses not to behave simply as customers, or interact with the world using advertising logos and applications, anger and frustration increases. And there is no longer any process or means of expressing our discontent or our collective intelligence and desire to transform the future.

My experiences and those around me tell the same thing: lives are getting faster, harder, more impoverished, depressed, and disenfranchised. This isn't inevitable, and it certainly shouldn't be acceptable, even if at present many continue to consent to the dreariness of everyday life because of a lack of credible alternatives. But the support and ideas that sustained those in the past to think beyond themselves are receding – political utopianism, social democracy, even the more problematic Victorian notion of 'public' in its libraries and parks are all in decline. The cultivated self has been traded in for the consumer-demographic individual. Online profiles, video games, and other kinds of recorded data have abstracted the self into individual data. Alternative spaces of reflection, the sacred or the profane, that might instil a feeling of empowerment through religious or political awe are disappearing. Food is the final object empowered with superstitious notions that might fundamentally alter our essence. Count the calories. As the tides of history recede some stragglers use their day-off to prospect for evidence of a missing future, possible but not at this moment, not for us at least. Our negation and alienation by financial capital extends to all aspects of our personal lives, whose value and fixity is seemingly in its capacity for productive output. Exhausted and fed up, the touch of a lover feels like a trespass of tensed-up skin, friends go unseen for months, one is barely capable of looking after even oneself in a bedsit and a meal for one.

Describing all this within one relation of 'negativity' is intentionally overambitious, but the originality and necessity of making this argument is that it acknowledges that each of us do not know all the answers; that indeterminacy, doubt and unfixed status are the only definitive status of contemporary experience; that insecurity is a political condition, one that like poverty can be left behind through collective revenge and violent strategic activity. It may seem that there are too many chaotic and contrary forces across the world to suggest one overarching and singular descriptive framework like 'negation' – even a term like 'system' seems tenuous, implying that a single and stable network of relations exists between all individuals, as if everybody could all share one language, one culture, or one standard mode of behaviour. But all life has been linked together and permeated by one universal relation, something which has entirely made and defined our sense of reality, be it in psychological terms, social terms, cultural, economic or other – organised capital. All forces are globally engaged in a single language expressed in the trade of shares, commodities, bonds, properties, resources, hours, and votes. These have been exchanged often by a small number of stable currencies with one overarching and universal currency. For the first half of the 20th century, this was British pound sterling; in the latter half, the US Dollar. Capital is now the shared language of all political and economic forces, the base language of life. Capital has enclosed all aspects of life, so that even the unknown, the imagined and the theological – all that was unthinkable to previous eras – can be measured within the language of money. Opportunities to escape financial Capital's enclosure of reality have on the whole disappeared. The wild and the weird are endangered, partitioned off into poverty or mined into for hipster marketing strategies.

Forces within neoliberal capitalism seek their own continued existence and self-perpetuation, in keeping with genetic and cultural imperatives throughout human history. In industry, the drive for factory and business owners to increase their wealth by maximising profit – by reducing labour costs and increasing or refining modes of production through industrial techniques – is called capitalism. Business and factory owners generate profit through the manipulation of their capital: the possession of labour, workers; the private ownership of the means of production – factories, mines, and so on; using increasing scales of machinery, factory, quantities of workers to forcibly organise social life around the factory. Finally, the capitalist would receive a great deal more of the wealth return of the product than any of the workers. This organisation of social and political life around economic production has determined the lives of our grand-parents and parents, establishing economic production as the principle activity and active principle of human societies in the West.

What has transformed in the last fifteen years is the means in which capital operates. The factories and mines have largely closed down, as have the industrial-scale public services and bureaucracies that existed around them. This isn't disappearing – it's simply shifted to cheaper sites in China and India. The heavy regulation of social life has also seemingly waned. Divorce, diversity and creativity are now clichés of our era. Working hours and sites of labour have melted into the home laptop and any public place with Wi-Fi internet. New cottage/bedsit industries are emerging in marketing and graphic design. In turn, capital has become increasingly productive. Whilst the public finances of nation-states stagnate into further debt and tax breaks, private corporations and their extremely high-paid CEOs are increasing their returns. The costs of production continue to shrink: for labour, workers are replaced with interns, wages are frozen and pension schemes cancelled; for production, overheads are reduced as desks are sold and factories, shops and offices closed down. Economic production becomes abstracted to online computer-based exchange. Unlike the factory, the computer and one's work emails are open and available at all hours. The traditional definition of 9-5 disappears, as managers are driven by *their* managers to drive workers to increased productivity, resulting in longer working hours, carried out often furtively in one's spare time. Increasing stress, depression and anxiety are the existential cost of this aggressive speed-up of capitalism.

In the West, capitalism described how wealth-owners and traders generated wealth privately. Increasing labour forces in turn organised themselves into trade unions, and demanded a fairer share in the profits of their own produce, political representation, equal employment rights, and a basic quality of life – meted out in welfare, pensions, annual paid holiday and so on. This conflict, predicted by Karl Marx as an inevitable internal implosion of capitalism that would lead to communism, instigated widespread social upheaval across the 20th century, in trade union disputes, race riots, and countercultural movements. Capitalists sought to increase their wealth-generation without the cost of labour or the threat of withdrawn labour. From the early 20th century onwards, political economists like Friedrich Hayek considered how capitalism could respond to the threat of organised communism in the form of the Soviet Union, as well as strong internal currents of dissent within the West. Neoliberalism became an idea where capitalists could overpower democratically-elected sovereign governments – sometimes composed of or responding to these socialist movements – by using unregulated financial exchange to determine the economic modes of production. This might seem like a removal of politics from economics then – surely deregulation meant that business could exist 'naturally', in an idyllic state free of the taint of political corruption? Instead neoliberalism became primarily a political gesture, led by politicians as a strategy to acquire full control over the conditions of labour. A pretty important gesture during an era of increasing trade unionism and independent thinking.

Political groups became disempowered by being unable to manage or regulate financial trade, which now determines as a single language most, if not all, human relations – a tentative claim in 1971, but a dreary but blatant conclusion after reading any newspaper forty years on. As political groups lost real economic power beyond tax-collection, capitalists could continue to fund political parties with donations in exchange for a say in policy or decision-making. Private funding and lobbying has also allowed sympathetic politicians to reach power, or reach a far wider media coverage, as the political cultures and classes of the US and UK demonstrate in cases like Rupert Murdoch, the Mittal scandals with Peter Mandelson, and many others.

Capitalists solved the irritating problem of labour: workers would have to train themselves, behave as what neoliberal theorists and management gurus call 'human capital', and perform as 'human resources' within their increasingly homogeneous organisations. A deregulation of pension and labour rights dreamt of by Reagan and Thatcher during the 1980s, but carried out with far more efficacy by Bush and Blair in the 2000s, achieved the desired management of labour. A more effectively managed labour force results in greater increases in profit-making, if not productivity. Stable employment, union representation, contractual working rights, paid sick leave and pensions become expensive 'luxuries' that politicians managed to opt workers out of, largely through additional legislative regulation. The irony is that whilst financial trade was deregulated from the 1970s to the present across the West, labour has been increasingly regulated.Increasing unemployment and underemployment has led to a gratitude complex where longer hours and more debasing tasks are lapped up with paranoiac relish. I must justify my position. If I stop working, the world might end.

Stress, anxiety and depression have risen across the capitalist world in response to this intensifying economic politic of capitalism. The World Health Authority now estimate that by

2020 depression will be the second biggest disease burden across the globe, whilst one third of all deaths by adults aged 15-44 across the world are suicides.[2] This isn't just a charity's Armageddon image of damaged refugees in some African state or ruined region of Afghanistan either. In London, suicide and deaths of undetermined intent are the single biggest killer of young men – 119 in 2010, and likely to rise – more than both violent assault or road traffic accidents put together.[3] Young people are living through the contradictions of this economic politic and now carry the scars and bruised knuckles of boredom, debt, unemployment, lack of shelter, having too many pressures to have happy relationships, or few places of support or community to now draw on. They have nothing. No commons to draw on. No cause to champion, no nation or national team to support (the cultural impact of neoliberalism and the pursuit of money above all else is clearly visible in the decline of British football over the last thirty years into Sky TV, mediocre and overpaid players, and overpriced, underwhelming matches). Even the future, that pasture of the American dream and countless others, has been deleted or postponed into infinite abeyance. As Kafka puts it, there is 'plenty of hope, an infinite amount of hope – but not for us'.[4] A five or six-figure debt will take decades to repay.

Quality of life is something anyone interested in happiness will desire. A truism of course, but let's unravel how quality of life operates. This involves, as philosophers and psychologists have variously explained, shelter, access to clean water and food, a peaceful and stable society, a sufficient distribution of roles or employment, health, friendship/altruism, and opportunities for education, religion and culture for self-fulfilment and relaxation. Quality of life is largely denied by the economic politic of neoliberal capitalism, as the single drive to increase wealth privately causes ecological, social and political damage – holes in the O-zone layer, increased poverty and unemployment, political destabilisation and irrelevance of democratic government. Quality of life should then become the point at which the subject of change is broached. Why? Capitalism certainly cannot guarantee a quality of life to the majority of the world's peoples. Evidence of economic and ecological exploitation clearly suggests that industrialised capitalism disadvantages and damages the mass of humanity.

One might then respond by asking: what's the alternative? There isn't an alternative. There cannot be an opt-out or exile from capitalism. The logic of economic enclosure of all life into abstracted capital means that all alternative spaces will eventually become commodified – think of the early 1970s counterculture, or the entrepreneurial development of black American hip hop from its initial social anger. Dissent at just a cultural level is safely self-nullifying to the financial power and arrogance of neoliberal governments. Instead of thinking about an alternative, there needs to be a decisive and determined move towards transforming life around us, and this has to be done on the level at which control and negation occurs – the political and the economic. This might use the language of quality of life and rational government to generate a new, regulated and global system of social democracy. The trade of resources and production would continue, channelled in a far more technologically and socially sustainable way. Political systems could be standardised and stabilised into representative and regularly-elected democracies with legally-binding global agreements on working rights, public control of infrastructure, production and management of resources and equality across social life. None of this is particularly radical. But when it is compared to the current political crisis of western governments and social life within the US and UK, it seems painfully idealistic. No historical event happens because it deserves to, because it should, for the sake of fairness or karmic return. Transformation must be acted out by a mass of agents, who lose their individuality by behaving as a democratic mass. This democratic responsibility is something required by all.

In this work I refer to a concept of constitution that is different to that known to American politics; and a concept of social democracy that is different to the political parties and historical movements that have gone under this name. Social democracy is not parliamentary, at least not in the corruptible national sense: it requires regular discussions by all, for all – that lead to regular democratic votes by millions nationally, as well as by majority locally (and rather than bemoan the fact that more vote in TV talent shows than general elections, instead recognise a possibility that democratic votes can involve all citizens, rather than a minority of overweight upper-class white public-school boys, the British political class). Cooperation replaces individual self-development as the overarching goal of the adult. The responsibilities and rights of adults could be defined clearly by a new constitution and social contract that imbues citizenship, a strategic goal I think is central to building a powerful alternative to neoliberal capitalism. At present this is idealism, and mass e-petitions reveal the danger of votes being manipulated for punitive and irrational restrictions on immigrants, Islamic 'terrorists', Traveller communities, and so on. In order for social democracy to function sustainably and peacefully, each person within the democratic body must be able to consent to social and political actions, requiring universal access to a sufficient level of education, critical thinking and compassion in each person, alongside a quality-regulated yet independent, not-for-profit media. It means a new social contract signed to ensure interest in cooperation, signed at adult age and validated by a legally-binding constitution, spelling out and defending in law the rights and responsibilities of the peaceful citizen and cooperative community. Locally, nationally and internationally, a legally-binding definition of citizenship can protect and empower human life to democratically pursue its social interests, collectively. Where idealism has failed, the power of the law and constitution can establish cooperation and social democracy as powerful and impermeable institutions.

Individually, there is little that could be done to alter anything. I am nothing. No, I am in fact a collection of mindless direct debits to a good cause, or I am that person wearing shoes or a jacket in a long line of young people queuing through a cold European city centre, late for work, or passively along for a corralled seasonal protest, or in a post office queue to send off a housing benefit claim that continues to be denied by impossible requests for imaginary documentation by agents who may or may not exist, empty assessors and data administrators who deny one's quality of life (the same assessors and data administrators one might become and work as for many years under temp contracts, cynically disinvesting oneself of any agency or utopianism about one's life. It's easier that way). Individually, no – very little. Expecting a democratic vote to meaningfully convey a political opinion or ensure fair local representation in the House of Commons is also meaningless – consider the last general election in the UK, where only 23% of the UK electorate voted for a Conservative Party candidate, who now lead the current political and economic strategy of the UK in the Coalition government.[5] (Of course no-one voted for the Coalition government, whilst one suggestion to increase local political representation – 'AV', the Alternative Vote – was also denied by voters in 2011, encapsulating the peculiar cynicism and political constipation of the British). And this 23% who seemingly got what they paid for with their vote are now being short-changed by various policy about-faces, egg-on-faces and an increasingly private government of the Prime Minister, Chancellor, and leading business and media figures. So, perhaps like a Kafka novel, the individual is entirely limited to never reaching what they desire.

Rather than write a psychological novel about negative

capitalism played out in the individual's tormented mind as the temptation might be, as it has been for Modernists since William Faulkner and James Joyce, I instead challenge the power of the individual to shape historical events. The individual worker is the one targeted and addressed by the citizenship of neoliberal capitalism – their right to spend and consume for themselves alone, offered in a social contract by debt. By instead behaving as a democratic mass who, through calculated organisation and cunning, target specific points of weakness and actively disrupt them, workers will gain a control and mastery over themselves and over the conditions of social life to rival and ultimately outmode the old destructive crisis politics of negative capitalism. The mass therefore need to disobey social conventions and disrupt the system of managed consent as I call it in the UK, the current set of social relations that make a disorganised mass of individuals seem like a 'society', as 'English', or 'British', 'western', 'white' or 'black', etc. This needs to be through a series of spectacular disruptions, for once as violent as the enforced poverty, lack of social care and ecological destruction wreaked on social life globally as an effect of capitalist modes of production. Examples include hacking, debt-strikes and tax-strikes, creating new local and national parliaments autonomously, community organisation, damage to financial sites of exchange, community 'supermarket sweep' competitions, and so on. The cheeky opportunism and genuine anger of the August 2011 teenage riots demonstrates the power of this approach. Political and economic systems cannot manage this chaos, particularly at a time when in order to maintain and maximise tax breaks on corporations and the wealthy, they have cut back staffing and funding in key social forces like social services, mental health teams, further education colleges, community charities, and the police. Governments and police no longer have the resources to manage or regain control of communities if they were to lose it. Here is an opportunity and a need for action. Not reaction, alternatives, voting for a Green politician, or direct debits to a good cause.

Disruption by a single mass of chaotic elements will tip the scales back towards democratic decision-making with maintaining and improving social life as the heart of its concern – social democracy. By being focused around a simple and strategic programme of goals like social democracy, constitution and citizenship, the democratic mass can remain united in the pursuit of civil war against neoliberal finance. Power cannot disappear, but it is neutralised when diffused among an equal mass of democratic agents who acknowledge only the rule of the collective, not the individual. Negative capitalism can be undone. It will lead to a greater disruption of social life and period of civil war initially, but the history of human societies demonstrates that cultures are fundamentally neither 'bad' nor 'good', as many moral critiques or defences of capitalism assume. Humans are not just dupes pre-programmed by genetics to conquer and destroy. Following chaos or trauma such as any major war, people do work together to solve problems collectively and generate new social and economic relations. It makes for less compelling polemic, but people enjoy conversation, friendship, and generosity far more than consuming or working. Think of the happiest people one personally knows of, and they share these traits.

'It is possible...but not at this moment': Kafka's utterance from "Before the Law" signals the stage in 20th century culture where the individual could no longer have confidence in knowing what was true, or having access to stable meanings or an under-standing of how the machinery of power operates.[6] It is also a succinct statement of the continual state of political abeyance and exception of the contemporary era – dreams of democracy are ground down in laptop-labour isolation, whilst explanations over the necessity or privatisation, the inability to access social support, even the loss of representative democracy are suspended in a new non-language of PR doublethink. It reminds us that individuals cannot hope that things will get better of their own accord, that capitalism will somehow sort itself out and happiness and positive engagement will replace the current condition of negation. Moral ideas of good and bad are redundant. Capitalism itself works very well: whilst labour sees its pensions, rights and health collapse, capital flows free, increasing in the hands of private CEOs, banks, and investment companies. The current political deadlock in the US and the Eurozone masks a tacit agreement between politicians and capitalists to stall and do nothing, thereby not interfering with the fundamental processes of neoliberal capitalism which have caused the huge debt crisis in these regions. Democracies have become redundant, their elected representatives deposed of like unfaithful colonial puppet leaders when financial capitalists decree in private decisions. Just as there should not be hope things will naturally stabilise, or politicians will suddenly see the light, there shouldn't be any assumption that social life will survive by doing nothing. Depression, suicide, poverty, irreversible environmental destruction and ill-health will continue to increase the longer no mass violent action is enacted. Here is one response.

2

Power versus Life: the Melancholia of Control

What are the strategies of the powerful today? Where are their weak-points? How can power be successfully contested and retaken by a democratic collectivity? Which strategies and directions could empower and most effectively channel the democratic exercise of power? Why has the Left hitherto failed to achieve a lasting victory against oligarchy and monarchy in the UK? When do 'we' start winning, and what actions are now required?

These questions are timely, yet political accounts since the early modern era have been defined with correctly applying and harnessing a power within life, be it the cunning of Machiavelli's Prince; the sovereign power invested in the body politic of Hobbes; or the power of life invested in the democratic multitude found in Spinoza's political writings. Power and life as separate and self-contained categories should at first raise suspicions: they can't be seen or tasted, and as singular concepts they are already embroiled in too many contradictory interpretations throughout history to have one agreeable definition. But both offer two powerful new ways of thinking through the contemporary problems of our time as a relation of tension. The argument in this chapter offers a theoretical explanation of the malaise and latent optimism which pulsates in every neurone and vein, which many of us feel at different moments.

Negative capitalism describes how capitalism has contaminated and recoded every aspect of individual and social life, abstracting all life into economically productive data. Even for the huge banks of unemployed 'reserve' labour, simply hanging around at home doing nothing or getting drunk offers an effective consent to the financialisation of everyday life into a boring series of expensive distractions. This occurred over two centuries ago in the wage relation generated by the industrial revolution in the West and the first urbanisation of workers from the countryside, a model of social development that continues to this day in China, India, and developing parts of Africa. Workers traded their time for money, a value which could then be exchanged for food, shelter and commodities. The more recent sign of change is the end of the fixed work contract and workplace, so that the modern worker now labours at most waking hours of the day, and not in a factory or farm, but at any place with electricity and internet access – cafés, pubs, most often at home. Lacking a contract, workplace and increasingly lacking even payment, the modern non-worker is increasingly expected to perform overtime and in their own time, re-training, ostensibly acquiring new skills and completing unrealistic assignments amidst increasing pressure to achieve goals and demonstrate the value of one's employment. Precariousness makes for more productive labour.

This kind of exploitative labour isn't itself new either, and marks the decline of the organised trade union movement in the 21st century, but the way capital has embedded itself within the heart of all our basic activities is new and significant – from sleeping to work, from infrastructure and communal facilities to stressed out psychological states, or from how resources are used or the basis of public conversation to contraception and when or if to have children. Nor is this arrogant western angst, as English-speaking call-centres operatives and skilled info-workers of India and China may testify. Wealth, money, assets, property – I prefer to simplify all this as capital – is striving to enclose all human life and animal life within its homogeneous economic sphere. The economic has become the overriding regulator of life, and economic profit the fundamental motive of politicians, military leaders, religious figures and business leaders. It's banal to say that capital can 'buy' whatever it wants, or that money makes the world go round. Far more simply, power is primarily exercised by capital and economic activity, all that which drives and determines the conditions of existence. This relation is what I mean by power against life. It's a deceptive simplification however: life is power, and power is an inescapable relation between all living things. At present, all life is managed on the basis of economic activity, for financial capitalism, something which itself negates and damages life. Defining the social basis of life just on the production and satis- faction of basic needs is obviously inadequate, and most of us seek something more than just eating groceries and paying the rent in our own lives. But this is how power comes to be wielded by life against its own interests, as life accepts a mean deal from financial capitalism in exchange for a very basic level of economic security. Social democracy emerges as a new kind of power which life can pick up and use towards its own sustainable and optimistic realisation. But until then, power is concentrated in the economic language of financial capitalism, and operates against life.

This chapter introduces and explores contemporary theoretical engagements with neoliberal capitalism, drawing on thinkers that will be familiar to some and new to others: Deleuze, Foucault, Hayek, Harvey, Marazzi, Negri and Pasquinelli. If the reader is already well-versed in neoliberal theory and current left-wing discontents, then feel free to skip ahead to Chapter Three. Through a discussion of Deleuze's theory of 'control', itself fashioned as a successor to Foucault's 'disciplinary societies', one can see how power and its techniques have powerfully come to shape cultural studies and critical theory since Foucault and Deleuze. This leads us to contemporary theoretical discussions of biopolitics and cognitive capitalism, where this contestation of power/information (what Deleuze conceives of as 'control') against life (the intervention and regulation of is what Foucault describes as 'biopolitics') runs through the recent arguments of Pasquinelli, Agamben, Virno, and Galloway. In all accounts, power is the essential: so let's begin by trying to name and account for power, beginning with Deleuze.

'The key thing is that we're at the beginning of something new', so Deleuze announces in his May 1990 "Postscript on Control Societies".[7] According to Deleuze, in or around May 1990 techniques of power changed. The old power-structures described as 'disciplinary' by Michel Foucault, exercised through disciplinary institutions, had given way to modulating networks of what Deleuze termed 'control'. Whereas discipline was located in specific sites, timetables and series of gestures, control as a form of power permeated throughout all times, all spaces, through diffusive networks of information. Control societies are 'free-floating', marked by new technologies such as the computer and information technology. Money and the metaproduction of finance replace wealth and wages, whilst workers are dissolved into 'dividuals' lacking interiority and driven to compete with one another in an endless CV-tournament of precarious virtuosity.[8] Media, PR, finance and services replace the production of goods, information or representative politics – as Deleuze puts it, 'Marketing is now the instrument of social control'.[8] Deleuze saw control as replacing disciplinary power, diffusing through disciplinary sites like the factory, school, clinic, hospital, family, pervading and constituting a field which no longer threatens death but regulates life, regulates sanitation and order, and what Foucault came to call 'biopolitics'.[9] Disciplinary power is a 'micro-physics' of power which describes the sum of relations within a field; a power which 'is exercised rather than possessed', treating the body individually through a subtle coercion of movements and practices.[10] Such a modality of 'uninterrupted, constant coercion' codifies and organises all time, space and movement, a power form based on the negation of work, time, space, identity and political agency.[11]

The account is unusually short, facilitating a wealth of interpretations, but Deleuze in fact offers a fairly specific account of
how this new type of society, the 'control society', operates.
Control is a productive form of power, with its own history, logic
and programme. Control describes a new form of power beyond
'disciplinary societies', a power that exists outside the old institutions of discipline in what Foucault calls the classical age – the
family, factory, army, prison, hospital, madhouse.[12] It is 'free-
floating', marked by new technologies such as the computer and
information networks, through finance, and Deleuze offers
further examples of nuclear technology, genetic programming, or
pharmacological treatments in psychiatry as opposed to the institution. Whilst such a power is now free of disciplinary institutions, its manifestation and exercise of control is far more subtle
and 'digital'.[13] It infuses all life through these networks,
'modulating' and indeed 'gas-like', a curiously thermodynamic
image of a diffusive power-form which is elsewhere described as
cybernetic, mediated no longer by persons with signatures but by
machines with passwords and codes.

To grasp this sprawling sense of control, consider it as a new
form of power no longer embodied in the authoritarian sovereign
or disciplinary institution, but now groundless, exercised
through vast networks of information and finance, in a sense
unaccountable in that no one person or institution mediates it.
Control is a form of power which dissolves time and space into
an endless present, liquefying labour and leisure into continuous
productivity, with the old timetabled and location-specific sites
of the disciplines bleeding out and permeating into all social life.
But this dissolution does not mark the end of the school as closed
site, or factory as closed site; instead control leads to a continuous
exercise of power, mediated through communication
technologies. Media, Public Relations, finance and services
replace the production of goods, information, or representative
politics – what Foucault described as a perfection of the juridico-

epistemological ranges of disciplinary power.[14]

Yet the problem with offering 'control', 'disciplinary' or even 'power' as descriptions is that although they conceptually simplify and structure power-systems, they offer little information about how these systems actually work. Analyses of control end up becoming exhausted in their own rhetoric. Instead neoliberal capitalism, incorporating the disciplines, control and much else, can be understood under the wider heading of negative capitalism, wherein life becomes negated by capital in both an ontological and socio-economic sense. This happens through a process of permeation of life by control technologies, primarily communication and information technologies, as Deleuze has so far outlined. It is an intimate diffusion and viral corruption of life by capital, deleting its potential and recoding it into a subject and agent of productive behaviours. There was no clear event when life suddenly became a subtle instrument of productive capital, a tool in its economy of crisis, but a slow and gradual seduction. By understanding why financial capital is the only meaningful political language of our era, the neoliberal era, a better understanding can be formed as to why democratic and socialist movements have been in terminal decline across the West over the last twenty years.

Control is a highly abstract way of thinking how power works, but it introduces the specific signs of how political and economic power operate at the end of the 20th century. Control's model is the business, which has replaced the factory and its disciplinary body of waged workers with a new ideology of competition, rivalry and motivation: 'in fact, just as businesses are replacing factories, *school* is being replaced by *continuing education* and exams by continuous assessment. It's the surest way of turning education into a business'.[15] This continuity of control leads inversely to uncertainty, unfinishability and the condition of precarity, of a loss of stability and grounding. Deleuze has a term for this ontological negation. He describes it

33

as a loss of interiority, so that the individual now becomes a 'dividual', no longer linked to matter but, like finance, free-floating, abstracted. Although it doesn't occur to Deleuze, the mass of dividuals share a hollowed-out and technologically-gifted identity, one no longer bound to old ideas of nationality or difference. A dangerous and exciting political potential emerges out of this negated army with nothing whatsoever to lose, containing nothing, and being no-one. One's subjectivity is no longer rooted to something within, but has now also untangled into a schizoid mosaic of faces – the Latin origin of the term 'individual' comes from something that is not (*in-*) divisible (-*dividuus*). The thinkers of the Italian leftist group the Red Brigades had already developed the term 'dividual' eight years prior to Deleuze, and for Renato Curcio and Alberto Franceshini, the city becomes an intensively organised 'penal colony' by computerized networks of control, stalked by surveillance, and where in 'the ideology of control, an at-risk dividual is already synonymous with a 'potential terrorist madman''.[16]

Contemporary London is one such city of intensive surveillance, random stop-and-searches and continual advertisements demanding obedient behaviours. Critiques of capital based on diminished existential experience are familiar: think of Herbert Marcuse's 'One-dimensional man', and Nina Power's more recent 'One-dimensional woman', both politicising the personal in their critiques of societal pressures for consumerism and conformity.[17] What makes Deleuze, Curcio and Franceshini's notions of an existentially diminished and alienated individuality unique is how loss of existential substance becomes attached specifically to post-Fordist economic policies and social affects. The dividual is free-floating, abstract like the financial dollar when US President Richard Nixon terminated the Bretton Woods agreement on 15 August 1971, marking the shift to supply-side economics of financial money production beyond Fordist manufacture. The source of global stability was no longer the US dollar and its fixed convertibility to gold, which had underwritten a whole field of further exchange rates. The US dollar instead became a fiat currency, valued now on financial speculation, US military hegemony, and the access of client states and its own working-class to cheap credit. The individual was no longer earthed to a fixed gold standard, but floated now as an abstracted financial value, her or his corporeality, collectivity and agency entirely negated.

A compelling vista of a dreary dystopia. The modern non-worker in a control society is a non-person, lacking interiority, defined by their debt and their (in)ability to compete with other workers, by their assimilation into new labour and consumption networks organised by computers. The mass too, so historically significant for Walter Benjamin in his visions of consumer-fascism, is too abstracted into 'banks', data samples.[18] This is a system of control that pervades the body like an evil 'IBM machine' through language: Deleuze takes his term 'control' from William Burroughs' *The Soft Machine*, where time is evacuated and uncoiled through sensory derangement,

> I felt the crushing weight of evil insect control forcing my thoughts and feelings into prearranged molds, squeezing my spirit in a soft invisible vise ... After some hours the invisible presence withdrew—I had passed the first test.[19]

'Control' is both terrifying yet over-stated, and perhaps it is the comparison to novels that make such realities still conceivably fantastical – places one can imagine but only elsewhere (think of how every time a new statistic appears on CCTV usage the same exhausted comparison to Orwell's 1948 novel *Nineteen Eighty-Four* is offered, when contemporary techniques of control are far more insidious and diffusive than Orwell's vision). Control is ultimately an entirely abstracted form of capitalist power, one where the old distinction of labour-capital in production is dissolved: businesses alone possess a 'soul', Deleuze tells us, and the production of goods has been replaced by the 'metaproduction' of services and money.[20] Life becomes both a product and productive of power, thus interweaving together control and biopolitics. The error is to assume that citizens became controlled clients without any kind of consent, that some great trick occurred and 'we' were all duped, and now await a saviour to reveal the truth. Power has pervaded life through offering great benefits – shelter, access to desirable goods and identities, empowerment. It's enjoyable, and without any credible alternative, a permissive cynicism creeps in where money makes the world go round, where ecological destruction isn't something worth worrying about if humans are going to die out anyway, and where there's no problem with having every aspect of one's life digitised and recorded by surveillance equipment if you haven't got anything to hide. Is it a penal colony if none of the prisoners in fact want to leave? Power pervaded life through consent, creeping through the bourgeois soul and hollowing us out into abstracted customers, eyeing up bargains and reactionary politics. Neoliberal capitalism has institutionalised the modern worker.

Few are happy, but beyond a few intellectuals and dreamers there is no visible sign of an alternative. What would life outside a controlled city be like? Could the modern dividual cope with it, and learn to develop new skills and behaviours? Yes, I passionately believe so. The altruism, art, intelligence and cooperation required by a social democracy, where each person is accorded equal status, a living wage and opportunity to determine political decisions and the operation of their own communities, is possible and within grasp. The effect of control is to render a person infantile, petulant and bored: behaviours often visible in social care or education, wherever an adult is deprived of their agency and independence. Collectively the modern worker has been rendered infantile. The revolt beyond control and beyond the irrationality of the neoliberal era will take place in action. Power can only be regained by life in its action, in democratic communities of workers, students, the unemployed, and so on, meeting amongst themselves, identifying, agreeing and attacking sites of negative capitalism, and disrupting and enacting their own alternative and autonomous self-determination. No political party or military force can contain adults who determine their own course of life collectively.

Foucault's 1975 *Discipline and Punish* accounts for power as a field of relations that invests life. An idea like the 'soul' becomes something powerful enough to exist in its own right and determine psychologically and socially the conditions and experience of life. Foucault's task is to explain how the modern idea of the soul transformed techniques of punishment, which shifted from public torture and execution, a regulation of death, to discipline, imprisonment and rehabilitation through surveillance, a regulation of life. Such disciplinary techniques, tested in the prison, become paradigmatic of wider shifts in the strategies of power during the 18th and 19th centuries. Rather than being inflicted on the criminal, the blasphemer or parricide by the sovereign, power comes to be internalised and inscribed or disciplined on the body through a careful timetable of labour-related practices, hidden behind high walls, its justice concealed within the large bureaucratic apparatuses of its operation.[21] Power therefore 'leaves the domain of more or less everyday perception and enters that of abstract consciousness; its effectiveness is seen as resulting from its inevitability, not from its visible intensity; it is the certainty of being punished and not the horrifying spectacle of public punishment that must discourage crime'.[22] This is power internalised, diffused through disciplinary networks, pervading and constituting a field which no longer threatens death but regulates life, regulates sanitation and order, what Foucault later calls biopolitics.[23]

Again Foucault: 'The body now serves as an instrument or

intermediary: if one intervenes upon it to imprison it, or to make it work, it is in order to deprive the individual of a liberty that is regarded both as a right and as property'.[24] Foucault describes how a 'micro-physics' of power operates, so that power is something which is inescapable; which describes the sum of relations within a field; a power which 'is exercised rather than possessed' and which permeates all relations within a society.[25] It is power which produces a specific kind of knowledge, and hence in all accounts of power the modern subject cannot possibly escape her/his own position of domination and exploitation within them. Largely presaging Deleuze, Foucault describes such a disciplinary power as treating the body individually through a subtle coercion, through a series of movements and practices. This description of productive power, invested in life, offers a number of helpful ways to think through control and power. Foucault's account places into oppositional relation life and power in terms of biopolitics, which will shape readings of power thereafter. Deleuze himself was reflecting on this struggle of life against power before he generates the solution of the control society in his short work *Foucault*, where he argues that, as a result of biopolitics and biopower, 'life ... emerges as the new object of power'.[26] Based on these theories of power then, resistance to capitalist or fascist forces must therefore put itself on the side of life, so that life becomes the ultimate vitalistic standard for resisting oppression.

By thinking of this dialectical relation of life-as-power versus contrary and negative forces, a perspective opens up to defend quality of life and social democracy as standards against privatising enclosures of public property by financial capitalists. Life is our ultimate point of commons with each other and with other creatures in the world, overcoming the current collective condition of alienation and cynicism. Whilst the intrinsically self-perpetuating nature of biological life cannot be altered, the collective commons of life forces a defence and assertion of a more basic standard than economic production and development, that which would ultimately destroy all life in its hunger. This perspective will force an uncomfortable abandonment from the cool safety of cynicism. The time comes to learn that life is not intrinsically selfish, hostile and dangerous – as leading capitalists and their gurus maintain. This kind of cynicism prevents us from trusting a credible alternative. Nor is life harmonious, or made up of one magic stable essence or unity called 'Nature' or any of that tosh – one can immediately sense the dangerous use of a term like 'natural' when one recalls where ideas of naturally superior or inferior life have led to historically. Life is complex, but its quality of being and the sheer numbers of support for democratic, cooperative life can be the rallying call of the first defensive revolts to financial capitalism.

How might a politicised opposition of life to the power of neoliberal capitalism function? Life needn't be against power, not when life itself is an operation of power, at present directed against its own interests. Rather, the blinkers of neoliberal capitalism need to be removed from social life. Each of us must re-programme ourselves to think beyond the mean profit principle, anxiety and cynicism of the neoliberal era. Think of the term potential and potentiality. In neoliberal capitalism workers are restricted or negated from reaching their potential: collective self-determination, their ability to enjoy individually and socially harmonious existences, a fair share of the product of their labour. Capital extracts much of this potential into productive behaviours, with a concomitant internalisation of the neoliberal work mindset – workers increasingly work longer or harder and invest more of their social time and hopes for self-fulfilment into their labour – but capital and work cannot fulfil the need for generosity, stimulation, cooperation or creativity. Why should it? Self-fulfilment is the lie of work, with workers forcing themselves harder into often fundamentally unnecessary and profoundly stressful or very boring jobs. The supermarket cashier, the call-centre node, the cleaner, the retail assistant might find their work tedious, but are driven by idiotic managers who genuinely believe in the importance of their work. Many readers will have worked with such people. If negation is a denial of potential, then life's power must be found and expressed beyond work, and against capital. The malls and out-of-town super-markets that both employ and consume workers will be the sites of riots and new community democracies. In all cases workers have themselves become the means of production: capital's power has permeated the worker's emotions or minds: the customer service assistant and knowledge worker are two of the most common positions available to young workers in the West today. In the case of knowledge workers, labour is mobile, usually temporary and takes place at the workplace of the laptop and mobile phone, at any possible urban geographic location. Life therefore has far more opportunities than it had previously for a dangerous abstention and revolt from capital. Power is in fact the potential within life: the distinction should then be life-as-power versus capital.

This distinction has already been considered in more rarefied terms by the cutting edge of Italian Marxists reading Deleuze from the Autonomist tradition. These new accounts carve out a new political space from which democratic bodies might reclaim their potential to act as life, though the esoteric undertones in these accounts can jar against otherwise lucid economic analysis. Paolo Virno takes up Foucault's notion of biopolitics to account for labour as pure 'potential', an abstracted 'non-present' form.[27] Such a potential labour-form accounts for both physical labour, cognitive labour and affective labour; as Virno puts it 'Life lies at the center of politics when the prize to be won is immaterial (and in itself non-present) labor-power. For this reason, and this reason alone, it is legitimate to talk about "bio-politics"'.[28] Labour-power is abstracted to pure commercial potential, and biopolitics is therefore the potential of this potential. But this continuous potential for labour is extended by Virno later, when he argues that the boundary between labour-time and non-labour-time has diminished – this pure continuous potential means that, like Kafka's Castle officials, the modern worker is continuously demanded to be productive, in a position of endless potential to work, working from home for instance, as labour and capital dissolve as distinct categories. Life's potential is perfected through power, and Virno's account reverses biopolitics so that it emerges out of life's potential as labour-power, rather than the other way around.

Franco "Bifo" Berardi also develops this notion, again heavily drawing on Marx's account of abstractive labour in *Capital* and the *Grundrisse*. Bifo is less interested in biopolitics and life, and more interested in how neoliberal capital controls the worker through alienation. Inverting the life-power axis, Bifo describes how neoliberal alienates all life and soul into a 'thanato-politics' of 'semiocapitalism'.[29] Yet against the familiar catastrophilia of left-wing melancholy, this is not strictly an alienation of life by power, but instead an embodied possession, as neoliberal governmentality rejects what I call the Fordist social politic for a post-Fordist economic politic. Bifo later describes that the effect of neoliberalism is a widespread inhumanity, defined by global panic, depression, autism, dyslexia and a general paralysis of the will. This quote is indicative of his general Marxist pessimism:

> After having subordinated the working class variable, capital readies itself for its new, titanic enterprise: subordinating the entire cycle of human cognitive activity into an automated system that is cabled on a number of levels: the economic, technological, psychochemical – and perhaps in the future, also the biogenetic.[30]

If Bifo takes a more Deleuzian reading of disciplinary power in terms of cybernetic control by semiocapital, his is certainly the most fatalistic of recent accounts, ludicrously advocating mass suicide and general escapism, a call unfortunately echoing those of Baudrillard, Lyotard, and others.[31] If control explains how power has shifted to the management of information, biopolitics is inversely taken up by Giorgio Agamben to describe how life itself is productive of power, and therefore is the foundation of all politics, be it in the form of bare life (*zoe*) or life in common to beings (*bios*).[32] Biopolitics is therefore no recent invention, but appears alongside sovereign power wherever power seeks to incorporate bare life as a foundational element within its domain. Agamben offers a new reading of Foucault which seeks to combine his juridico-institutional accounts of power with the later theories of biopolitics and biopower, which Agamben reductively reads as technologies of the self, which also ignores Foucault's later biopolitical account of neoliberalism. In each case life both produces power and is objectified by it, so that politics becomes the site where bare life is 'humanised' through the *logos*, knowledge, and so in a sense becomes an object of power, of investment through power. Power becomes a play of these forces then, where limits of inclusion and exclusion drive us to a state of exception. Power now permeates and realises an even more insidious control of all life.

Perhaps Michael Hardt and Antonio Negri are most faithful to both biopolitics and control in their account of *Empire*, whilst offering a specific account of a counter-empire which can use its life to affirm its own power. They specifically offer a definition of biopower as a situation where 'what is directly at stake in power is the production and reproduction of life itself'.[33] Power entirely permeates the bodies of the population, producing life itself, and in perhaps too-perfect fit, 'only the society of control is able to adopt the biopolitical context as its *exclusive* terrain of reference'. Empire, the name for this figuration of power, becomes the absolute inversion of life into capital, one where subjectivity – what disciplinary societies had been composed to produce – is now rendered a 'non-place', one where the subject is now encoded, negated and abstracted into the virtuality of Empire's networks of control. Hardt and Negri optimistically return that living labour, life contained within the potential of the multitude, has the power to resist capital and reclaim the future, an argument also generated and supported by Alexander Galloway and Eugene Thacker, who articulate life as a 'sort of counterpower'.[34] The limit of this argument is that revolution and resistance become even more abstracted than financial capital, described often explicitly in directly religious terms. Although Galloway and Thacker are a little more nuanced, they too offer a tabular comparison of contemporary societies of control with a mystical '...the Future', whereby our contemporary mode of liberation, 'neoliberal capitalism', is now replaced with ' "life-in-common"'; its historical actor being no longer 'communities; the people' of control societies but the 'multitude'.[35] Such arguments although curious give no practical insight or genuine strategy of resistance, and facilitates the further abstraction of capital with a mystified description of resistance as 'life' itself.

Although life and power are a useful way of thinking through these concepts, simply returning to 'life' and hoping to find a defence within it itself, without reversing or challenging how networks of power diffuse through it, is at best escapist and at worst utterly complicit in the processes it might challenge. Christian Marazzi's innovative account of contemporary neoliberal capital also draws on this life-power axis to offer a conception of 'biocapitalism'.[36] Marazzi describes how the entire 'financialisation' of social relations by capital, in a similar form to the 'potential' discussed by Virno above, has rendered life itself as an object of capital. Using the most recent capital crisis of 2008, Marazzi argues against a socialist position that would assume that this crisis marks the ultimate excess-point of capital accumulation. No, instead this financialisation represents a perverse new kind of accumulation, whereby the body is no longer an instrument put to use as work (labour), but becomes instead the object itself of capitalist accumulation – biocapitalism. It is a catchy yet hollow phrase in Marazzi's otherwise unsatisfying account, and he offers only a few tentative scraps of the 'Google model' of web 2.0, free labour and precarity which are acquirable in more insightful and didactic detail elsewhere. Marazzi describes how this biocapitalism works beyond the old direct productive processes, becoming an apparatus in precisely the way Foucault and Kafka envision power.[37] The old wage-time of work is undone by a new culture of internships and volunteering encouraged into the increasingly scarce job market, a new kind of 'virtuosity' (to use Virno's term) of self-commodification.[38] Similarly power pervades life in the new information networks which render us productive working subjects, accessible at all times and in all locations, flattening the disciplinary dimensions of separate time and space into a continuous control, a continuous working time and working location (particularly if work occurs at the same place where one lives). The fields of informational labour and the affective labour of service-work converge here for Marazzi and Pasquinelli too, as cognitive capitalism and biocapitalism come together in the production ultimately of life and of affect.[39] Capitalism ultimately negates the independent status of the worker, who must have their entire personal lives, thoughts and emotions at the service of production.

Marazzi describes this new post-Fordist parasitic capital as 'a totality of immaterial organizational systems that suck surplus-value by pursuing citizen-laborers in every moment of their lives, with the result that the working day, the time of living labor, is excessively lengthened and intensified'.[40] The description of a living labour as a 'conscious organ' from Marx's *Grundrisse* has been very important for the Italian Autonomist movements, particularly with the idea of a 'general intellect' of labour which holds a more specific power than the Marxian notion of class consciousness.[41] A comment by Marx in his 1844 manuscripts is insightful into this description of life as productive of labour:

> The increasing value of the world of things continues in direct proportion to the devaluation of the world of men. Labor doesn't only produce commodities; it produces itself and the worker as a commodity—and does so in the proportion in which it produces commodities generally.[42]

Is this life-power axis always invariably a struggle of labour against the commodity and capital? Whilst some accounts wrestling with Deleuzian control advocate a somewhat childish escapism of pure life out of labour, a monastic and pure abstinence in Tiqqun, Bifo and others, there is finally a sense of life's purposiveness in Matteo Pasquinelli's bestiary of contemporary capital, *Animal Spirits*. And whilst Marazzi, Virno, Bifo, Hardt and Negri all attempt to offer a notion of the *common* as a site of affirmative resistance for the multitude, an embodiment of free life, Pasquinelli cleverly twists this 'potential' into something altogether more seditious against capital. If power and control are to be undermined, this can only be through a 'creative destruction' which cannot be recuperated into capitalism or the forged consent of representative democracy.[43] Pasquinelli offers the more fundamental point that contemporary accounts of biopolitics are in danger of inflating power into a hyper-vague abstraction that leads ultimately to a new puritanism, becoming nonsensically vague ('we are for *life*, against *power*').[44] Foucault demonstrates that there is no complete 'escape' out of the field of power relations, whilst Pasquinelli directs his readers (which he presumes are anti-capitalist) to avoid the three mistakes of the contemporary Left: firstly, to assume the natural goodness of human beings or life, that through the right conditions will overthrow its chains – an error of reasoning he associates with Chomsky and his followers. Secondly, that the Left lacks a proper coherent economic analysis, leading to the third problem that invariably protest groups target obscure weak-points, such as global conferences in peripheral towns. The inevitable failure of the Left leads to resentment and cynical fatalism. Whilst Marazzi is unfortunately unique among contemporary critics of neoliberal capitalism for offering coherent economic analysis, note the significance that both Deleuze and Foucault (in his later 1978-9 lecture series) turn to describing power relations in economic terms – Foucault's course in biopolitics becomes the most coherent excavation of neoliberal theory to date, whilst Deleuze's control societies cannot be understood without reference to post-Fordism. Yet in both cases ultimately economic terms and power systems lack clear conceptual definition, and instead the reader is given 'control' or 'disciplines', some unclear instructions and left to unpack the rest – Ikea theory for an Ikea generation.

Pasquinelli envisions a resistance to neoliberal capitalism based on the power of the 'biomorphic unconscious', a term that might be pulled straight out of the writings of Georges Bataille, which harnesses the violent animalistic excess of immaterial and cultural production labour against capital.[45] In this move, life is now invested into technology as a form of resistance to power, what he later ingeniously calls a 'zoopolitics' of *zoe* replacing biopolitics, where energetics replace aesthetics. Pasquinelli relishes the animalistic and evil connotations of this dark matter, but like Virno and Negri he fails to recognise that this zoopolitics simply restores a religious conflict of light against dark into the world, with this time rebellious angels (or 'libidinal parasites') taking on Manichaean proportions. As Pasquinelli argues,

Collective intelligence is the ambivalent exoskeleton of the species: at once the basis for *institutions of the common* and an extension of humanity's inborn aggressiveness ... a *bicephalous* nature of politics, where the biological evil is part of the institutional good, where *logos* travels always with its own peculiar *hubris*.[46]

Such a conception might work as a powerful metaphor for irrational acts of violence against capital, be they looting, rioting or otherwise, but such a term might be applied easily to any antisocial behaviour without a clear sense of why and how it is constituted as a political act of life. This anti-capitalist 'unconscious' still fundamentally assumes a dormant vitalism that will erupt against its codifying capitalist control, yet such a resistance against neoliberalism, the information technology revolutions and the continued immaterial permeation of negative capitalism has yet to arise, despite its many Cassandras and prophets announcing its imminent downfall. If, as Pasquinelli tells us, echoed by Lazzarato, Hardt and Negri, each of us lives in the midst of an 'immaterial civil war', then what kinds of weapons might be identified for cognitive workers in Canary Wharf, for fast-food workers in the service-stations of the M25, for data-chip factory assistants in China's Guangdong Province? Little strategies emerge apart from a similar gloomy image, a strange cynicism of the Left that ultimately restores the old authoritarian passivity of the wise scholar-doomsayer, the passive audience/ motivated subject. It leads to the ultimate buffoon of the sad fair capitalist, like Nick Clegg, expressing remorse and tender feeling in regard to the expediency of his decisions.

The profound problem with offering 'control', 'disciplinary' or even 'power' as descriptions is that although they allow us to conceptually simplify and structure power-systems, they offer little information about how these systems actually work. Talk of control ends up exhausting its own rhetoric, falling back into the morass of left-wing downfall porn peddled by wrinkled cynics with nothing new ever occurring. Deleuze makes a peculiar remark at the end of the "Postscript" about the need for young people to be motivated, without ever asking for what this motivation occurs.[47] In the middle of crisis and negativity, what is motivation? Motivation marks the point of collusion and possible subversion by life against power. After all, being a 'motivated' candidate is just another unwritten rule of temporary jobseeking, alongside being 'dynamic', or that of 'liaising' rather than talking, another sleight of hand term that should irritate and insult the intelligence of anyone who hears it. What does being 'motivated' mean? It is the old-school tie, a lie uttered that consents to the empty facts of the CV-factory of precarious employment. It is not motivation but desperation: unlike Deleuze's generation, young people are mostly underemployed or unemployed, and those that are in work are exhausted by the sheer level of productivity demanded of them. This isn't being motivated, but being made to fight and lie and deceive to achieve a basic existence. Neoliberal capitalism effects a control of place, time and subject through a crisis within the subject, allowing negativity and cynicism to hollow us through and through. Life will regain its power through use of cunning, intelligence and strategy.

3

Neoliberalism; Or, the Economic Politic of Negative Capitalism

Any account of politics or economics has to consider the perspective of those who are powerful, those working at the helms of neoliberal capitalism in finance, politics, PR and business, and must consider their reasons and ideology for justifying their own objectives. Slavoj Žižek notes that a ruling ideology can only operate by incorporating some of the authentic longings of the subjugated majority, whilst keeping this content in balance with the specific hegemonic interests of those forces of domination.[48] The following three chapters explore how neoliberal capitalism has permeated social life, abstracting all social relations into financial ones, and how a new language of speed, freedom, and security has satisfied popular desires for control whilst reinforcing anxiety and depression – how, in short, these two particular contents Žižek describes can work in tandem. First however, the term neoliberalism requires explanation.

Neoliberalism describes a range of political and economic theories and practices that believe that free economic trade and exchange is the guarantor of individual and political freedom. In its contemporary theoretical guise, it developed in central Europe and the United States from the 1920s onwards, avowedly anti-Keynesian and anti-Communist, and reaching prominence in the post-WW2 construction of West Germany into a neoliberal state founded primarily on economic rather than social functions.[49] Through the influence of Friedrich Hayek and the Mont Pèlerin Society established in 1947, neoliberal theories developed from the 1960s-70s pervaded through corporate and capitalist economic restructuring, a process of 'neoliberalization'.[50] Neoliberalisation as political practice developed from 1976, and arose in response to a complex web of economic problems from declining production, rising oil prices, the collapse of the Bretton Woods agreement fixing the US dollar to the gold standard, spiralling inflation and increasing political resistance and labour militancy.[51] As David Harvey and Marazzi analyse, it has led to a financialisation of cultural and social life: the privatisation of public utilities, welfare and social housing, nature (via intensive agriculture), information and intellectual property rights – affecting all aspects of social life and mounting to a mass dispossession as economies became transformed towards the pure production of financial wealth.

Neoliberalism should be considered as both a political and an ontological event in late modern capitalism. It informs Deng Xiaoping's economic liberalization of Communist China towards capitalist production; Margaret Thatcher's election in order to "Get Britain working", solve stagflation and defeat militant trade unionism in May 1979; Paul Volcker's takeover of the US Federal Reserve in July 1979; and Ronald Reagan's aggressive Christian capitalism after election in 1980.[52] Although a state-managed practice, the state's official functions are limited to deregulating financial controls and trade barriers, control of inflation, the full privatisation of public enterprises, and opening up markets to foreign investment and expropriation. Its immediate cost was soaring interest rates and unemployment, causing Mexico and other states to default on their IMF loans; whilst under Thatcher forced industries into major decline and brought unemployment levels up to three million, with similar problems in the US.[53] It loosened Capital and allowed its process of accumulation to continue, leading to economies being based on 'supply-side' services and finance, rather than the production of goods, marking a shift from Fordism to deindustrialised post-Fordism.[54] Wealth becomes 'deterritorialized' and negated into instantaneous abstracted flows facilitated by a new information age of rapid communication technology and flexible capitalist accumu-lation.[55] The case of Iraq's neoliberal restructuring by its American occupiers in 2003 repeats an established pattern in West Germany from 1948.[56]

Foucault describes neoliberalism as an 'art of government' or 'governmentality': in each case characterised by a 'state phobia' that poses the freedom of markets to supervise states and determine the freedom of citizens.[57] As a governmentality, neoliberalism is an intensification of 19th century biopolitics, so that all life becomes abstracted and organised into quantifiable data, an economic politic, where populations are sufficiently disorganised enough to stall resistance. Nation-states manage their populations (and via neoliberal-influenced international organisations like the IMF and World Bank, their indebted client-state's populations) to sacrifice or negate public institutions, wages and working rights in order to feed further capitalist accumulation using a fear-based language of crisis, austerity, terrorism, emergency, and debt, fuelling their own power-bases – contemporary Greece is a most recent example. This leads Virno and Marazzi to define neoliberalism as a 'communism of capital', one where capital flows free, even if labour is increas-ingly tightly regulated, abstracted and negated into non-labour, unpaid labour.[58] An entirely meaningless language of 'freedom' is used to justify the rights of bankers or mining companies to extract increasing profits and productivity from exhausted ecosystems and individuals. The celebration of the 'Big Society' (implying inversely a small state) marks the PR-redefinition of the state from cradle-to-grave provider of the old social politic, to a lean, war-making and business-propping elite of public school boys. The move in Britain towards police commissioning, GP-commissioning and compulsory independent academy status for failing schools since 2011 onwards sets the state up to fail: for instance, GPs will find it difficult to accurately and effec-tively commission local healthcare services, which will then require the private sector to come in and 'rescue' run-down services, receiving a great deal of public wealth transferred to them, with services wrecked by being twisted to make private profit. The privatisation of British infrastructure during the 1980s is the case in point of why privatisation is a sustainable and desirable option for the wealthy; and why if no violent opposition is mounted, these encroachments on civil life and well-being will continue unabated.

The irony of neoliberalism is that it doesn't involve free markets at all. It has historically required specific intervention by governments or intergovernmental global agencies into the markets, forcibly deregulating them and transferring public property into private hands. It is maintained with regular state intervention, from continued sales of public assets or resources to regular bail-outs by governments of beleaguered companies or financial institutions. It is a state-imposed mechanism. Unlike Keynesianism, that other state-imposed regulator of wealth within and among states produced by 20th century idealism, the primary goals of neoliberalism are the continued production and accumulation of capital by a tiny elite and the disorganisation of trade unionism and socialism, that which might threaten this accumulation of wealth by the rich. Credit has been employed to produce this wealth in times of stagnant productivity, and offer workers a mirage of stable living standards, all the while their wages frozen and declining in real terms. Neoliberalism has been a major success in the West. Extremely high bonuses, unemployment, and wealth inequality are built into its blueprint, and the trade of financial capital is its shared language. This is not a time of capitalism in crisis, but capitalism in the full throes of its joyous existence. It will not be harmonised by a spectrum of interventions based on one's political preference – reform, regulation, riot, revolution, and so on – as many contemporary political commentators assume. If young workers do not like their poverty and anxiety, then contemporary political and economic structures informed by neoliberalism will need to be attacked and dismantled.

Neoliberalism as a theory functions as both apologist and facilitator of financial capitalism. Understanding neoliberalism in practice requires grasping the specific programme of deindustrialisation which began from the early 1970s and escalated during the 1980s, which emerged out of the state confrontations with trade unionism, improvements in technology rendering old forms of manufacture costly and obsolete, and the availability of cheaper goods produced overseas that ensured greater private profit for corporations in the Anglophone world. Governments and corporations encouraged the widescale dismantlement and/or privatisation of industries, such as docking, mining, and manufacture, and began instead basing new economic activities around financial trade and the service sector. Neoliberalism in practice developed at numerous points in the West but for clarity of argument the case of London offers a number of examples to illustrate general trends.

As the capital of a fading former empire, London was particularly blighted by the loss of its docking facilities and industries as a result of cheaper international competition and political attacks on unionised industries. Working-class Londoners had settled into relatively stable and reasonably-paid employment from the late 1950s, enjoying a quality of life unknown to pre-WW2 generations. With rising inflation and unemployment from the mid-1970s marking the end of this brief period of prosperity, a new era of credit, both internationally and locally provided, eased the decline of living standards for many in the capital. In the working patterns of Londoners, manufacturing, industry and docking have been largely replaced by office administration, retail and consumer services, finance, unemployment, and a growing informal economy of cleaners, mini-cab drivers, porters and security guards.[59]

Deindustrialisation in London began firstly with its iconic

docks on the Thames. Between 1967-71 almost all of London's dockyards closed, aggravated into decline and non-productivity by the effects of containerisation, which led to decreasing trade, improved facilities elsewhere, alongside and regular union walkouts.[60] Between 1966-76 over 150,000 jobs were reportedly lost in the Docklands' boroughs. This in itself amounted to 20% of jobs alone, but exacerbated an even wider and undocumented decline of small businesses and industries dependent on the trade of the docks.[61] By 1979 a government-TUC agreed compromise on wage freezes unravelled and union walkouts brought London's infrastructure to a standstill, encapsulated by monumental pyramids of uncollected rubbish bags. Anxieties about immigration and a sense of boredom, drabness and stasis were re-enforced by regular union strikes. The Conservative Party capitalised on this: advertising agency Saatchi and Saatchi supplied Margaret Thatcher's 1979 Election campaign with a winning slogan for disaffected middle-class and working-class voters: 'Labour Isn't Working',[62] whilst Thatcher described Britain being 'swamped' by its non-white citizens of the post-colonial Commonwealth.[63] The condition of London was radically transformed by Thatcher, who dismantled a post-war consensus about nationalised industries, the provision of welfare and council houses, London's own government body even, abolishing the Greater London Council in 1986, alongside cutting previously high expenditure on public services. As she announced at the 1977 Conservative Party conference: 'We do not believe that if you cut back what the Government does you diminish its authority. On the contrary, a government that did less, and therefore did better, would strengthen its authority.'[64]

The practice of neoliberal economic policies from 1979 onwards had three major identifiable effects that would exacerbate a new modernity in London: the decline of British Modernism in infrastructure and social housing, and the wider effects of privatisation and a decline in the notion of the public society; the move towards a 'flexible' information and finance-based economy, marked by the re-centralised development of Canary Wharf and the London Docklands; and finally the boom of the service sector and increasing personal consumption, with culture and style proliferating as capitalist commodity.

Exhausted by a second world war in less than three decades, the British government under Labour leader Clement Attlee began a massive process of economic restructuring. What emerged during this post-war "compromise" was the development of a modern welfare state and National Health Service. This was driven by a belief in Keynesian economics, which argued that social development could only be effectively guaranteed and maintained by public services and nationalised industries, not profit-seeking market forces.[65] Citizens would be cared for from cradle to grave, and they would be entitled to a better standard of living, better educational opportunities and a better quality of housing than their parents' generation.[66] In architecture and urban planning there was a utopian strand to develop a new future for the British working class. A particular kind of British Modernism in architecture – later to refer to itself as 'Brutalism' – became influential in designing new high-rise estates that promised fresher air, larger living spaces, core infrastructure (running water, heating, electricity) and improved amenities. These new "cities in the sky" were constructed across the UK from the early 1950s up until 1979 in places like Thamesmead, in south east London, which offered residents desperately in need of rehousing from the slums of south-east London a new '21st century town'.[67] These idealistic housing projects were however aggravated into decline by cheap construction, lack of maintenance, and often a lack of public transport connections, compounding the eerie sense of abandonment and a future aborted one experiences when walking through the British Brutalist estates.

If Thamesmead was built according to the socialist

modernism of left-leaning Labour politicians and social planners, its fate was transformed by another effect of Thatcher's neoliberal practice. "Right to Buy" legislation allowed council tenants to buy their own homes, often at greatly discounted rates, in effect privatising them in the same way nationalised industries were.[68] In the short-time many felt empowered and optimistic – the image of front doors with different colours became an icon of a Britain moving out of austerity, and DIY programmes and stores boomed from the late 1980s and throughout the 1990s. Individuals were encouraged to buy shares in previously nation-alised industries like British Telecom.[69] But privatisation also removed a great deal of the social housing stock. It forced housing prices to go up, to the gain of entrepreneurial property speculation that neoliberalism sought, but to the disadvantage of those in need of social housing. Since 1979 there has been a major decline in social housing construction. Left to the profit-seeking hunger of market forces, public services, housing and infra-structure decayed and fell into crisis, suffocated of public funding. Crime, unemployment and homelessness have conse-quently spiralled between 1980 and 1990, as the inner city continued to depopulate.[70]

An increasing fear of crime saw the exclusion of the outside, both in the rise of the gated community – private property devel-opments that excluded the outside – and in the comparable rise of metal security gates being attached over the front doors of working-class properties, particularly in housing estates. Rich and poor were installing metal gates to secure themselves inside their homes, increasingly the locus of leisure activities, attempting to exclude an increasing fear of crime but in effect providing a continual psychological reminder of their own vulnerability. Property speculation took on popular appeal, as TV programmes and lifestyle magazines from the 1990s celebrated the "property ladder" as a means of making money, buying dilapidated inner-city Victorian housing, restoring 'heritage' features and general superficial improvements, before re-selling again with often great profit.[71] This marked a more general thrust of 'gentrification' across London, as property prices and social housing shortages forced many working-class Londoners out towards the sprawling suburbs into often sub-standard accommodation, or homelessness altogether.

The process of deindustrialisation was completed by a process of financialisation of the Docklands, which by 1981 had entirely closed. As Michael Heseltine, then Secretary of State for the Environment, flew over the now de-industrialised docklands, he was struck by their physical decline and 'the need for urban regeneration', an essential mantra term for social inter-vention policy over the next 30 years.[72] He announced in public that the area represented 'a major opportunity for development that London needs over the last twenty years of the 20th century'; in private he was less optimistic, seeing in the 'rotting docks' a crumbling tip, or '6,000 acres of forgotten wasteland'.[73] Heseltine first established the London Docklands Development Corporation (LDDC) in 1981, declaring the area to be an 'enter-prise zone' with no promised tax rates on commercial and business properties for a decade.[74] By 1991 the entire area had unrecognisably transformed into a playground of skyscrapers, shopping centres, Legoland lakes, and champagne-spattered luxury high-rises. Thatcher's deregulation of the London Stock Exchange in 1986 removed currency controls and allowed inter-national financiers to trade, creating a short-lived "Big Bang" for this new finance-based economy. In accordance with David Harvey's theory of 'capitalist overaccumulation', much of this new profit accumulated by capitalist enterprise was surplus to contemporary demands, and was plunged into the conspicuous consumption of Yuppies, or invested in the built environment: US Bank Credit Suisse first proposed the huge Canary Wharf skyscraper, and Canadian firm Olympia & York took over construction, part-financing the impressive extension of the

Jubilee line.[75] Yet affordable housing and jobs for the older local communities had failed to materialise. In 1993 the rest of the Isle of Dogs, the largely working-class stub of a community left behind to the south of the Docklands regeneration site, acquired the honour of being the first London constituency since the Second World War to elect a fascist BNP councillor, who led a campaign blaming the indigenous Islanders' insecurities on incoming Bangladeshi immigration.[76]

The effect of neoliberalism has brought mixed fortunes to London – good for wealthy, city financiers, and bad for London's communities and working-class. Edward Soja describes well this condition of de-industrialisation and increasing social exclusion, poverty, as a 'metropolarity'.[77] A study by Barnardos published in July 2010 revealed that eight in ten children living in Tottenham, Poplar and Limehouse, Bethnal Green and Bow live in poverty – with a wider figure of 36 (primarily inner) London constituencies having over 50% of its children in receipt of the highest child benefit rate.[78] With no will or plan to reduce this poverty, one of the core issues of contemporary London is this increasing social polarity, exclusion and poverty. Equally concerning is a whole new kind of 'waning of affect' and 'depthlessness': not so much in the 'postmodern' sense intended by Fredric Jameson here, but in the passive acceptance and cynicism regarding such poverty by politicians and the public today.[79] In such a 'metropolarity', youth support services are stripped of funding, community centres close, disability, child benefit and carer benefits are cut, often through a bureaucratic re-classification, and Educational Maintenance Allowance payments cancelled, whilst very few in the media and political class are willing, or able, to account for this phenomena, and link it to the extraordinary rise in rioting and civil disobedience in the UK over the last 12 months.

In contemporary London there is no growing 'classlessness', as promised by Tony Blair and the New Labour project, but an increasing cynicism and fatalism in the population. Perhaps this is just the effect of Thatcher's declaration of the end of society and the decline of the public sphere? The huge increase in shopping malls, chain retail stores, and credit-fuelled consumption in the working-classes and the middle-classes have engendered a focus on commodities and self-image, whilst support for public welfare and wealth redistribution to the poor has declined since 1983, as the 2010 British Social Attitudes Survey reports, and which the following 2011 British Social Attitudes Survey found had solidified into a general hard-heartedness and civic indifference.[80] This is fairly predictable: it is not just poverty and scarcity that makes modern individuals more aggressive and violent to one another, but the effects of a wider decline of self-worth which comes with existential negation. In urban communities ruined by poverty, young people particularly feel little worth or value about their lives or prospects, a fair response to broken communal facilities, police discrimination, economic marginalisation, and a lack of credible alternatives or role-models. This lack of self-worth is expressed in empty acts of aggression, urban callousness and vandalism; it's also resolved in the peer-support affinities formed in local gangs or online gaming. Whilst anger increases the cynical distraction in commodities remains, and frustration is increasingly channelled like a thwarted desire into the modern neuroses of passive aggression and self-destructive violence. Hence why the target of the August 2011 riots were largely sports or electronics shops selling fashionable goods to young men which they can no longer access – and hence why little was actually stolen, and the real anger was expressed in violent acts against these sites.[81]

The vision of a ruined city is in danger of lacking the nuances, niches, wrong turns, heterogeneity and the pleasures of anonymity and alienated brutality that defines the experience of London. Like most economically active cities in negative capitalism, London is by and large a brutal and overpriced city, unkind to inhabitants and strangers alike, a glorious accident like all other parts of life. Some of us refuse to leave the place, and take consolation in observations like Doreen Massey's, that,

> amid the Ridley Scott images of world cities, the writing about skyscraper fortresses, the Baudrillard visions of hyperspace ... most people actually still live in places like Harlesden or West Brom. Much of life for many people, even in the heart of the First World, still consists of waiting in a bus-shelter with your shopping for a bus that never comes.[82]

This finally feels like the real contradiction of the 'modernisation' of Britain's neoliberal project – one or two modern structures in an otherwise deprived, bleak and boring landscape. A similar effect can be seen in Stratford today as a result of the Olympics: a PR event built with corporate sponsorship, tourism and property development in mind, involving the demolition and expulsion of settled communities with the empty and symbolic façade of 'regeneration' (a new sports centre, a brand new Westfield mall) that conceals the continued stagnation, deprivation and desperation of Londoners across the city. Negative capitalism has rendered the personal as biological, the cultural as political, and the social as economic. In approaching the failure of the 'future' as dreamed by socially progressive modernists, one can identify distinctly new cultural experiences like 'ruinporn', analysed later, and 'riotporn', the pleasure taken in watching violent images of riots and police confrontations on YouTube. These mark the point of ultimate passivity as spectacles of decay and destruction arouse viewers to contemplate in perverted form the end of capitalism, and the possible agency of the masses themselves – we ourselves – who momentarily become the object rather than subject of history. Explaining to ourselves and others that political acts and interventions could not carry any influence no matter how 'naïve' the avidity of our desire, cynicism signals a conservative inaction and truce with the state of things. On the Left, this is marked by an increasing reluctance to engage with local politics and community struggles in order to build a mass movement – "they wouldn't understand"; on the Right, by a reactionary culture of blaming political leaders for problems which are well beyond the power or interest of the British government. Either encourages inaction.

In a neoliberal society the only way each of us can keep up with the model of productive consumption, the last place of agency and meaningful choice in these times, is to get into hard debt. Which doesn't feel so bad when whole nation-states, companies, local councils and the majority of one's friends are doing exactly the same thing. The question then becomes: who exactly is all this money owed to? And why is *everyone* getting into debt when seemingly all goods, skills and services are already available?

4

Debt: An Idiot's Guide to Defaulting the Future

Negative capitalism generates its own ontological experience, embodied in Foucault's description of a new 'homo œconomicus', man as entrepreneur of himself, 'being for himself his own capital, being for himself his own producer'.[83] Gary Becker too abstracts social and family life into machinic 'human capital'.[84] Or think of that even more dreary contemporary term of 'human resources' in the modern corporation. The popularity of the BBC show *The Apprentice* with computer salesman Sir Alan Sugar gives the lie that each of us can make it big with the right amount of pluck and entrepreneurial determination. The general sleaziness, arrogance, and fundamental lack of social skills and intelligence of most contestants on this show demonstrate that the *homo œconomicus*, the man or woman of the neoliberal era, is a dangerous idiot. The show's contestants are entertaining rather than inspirational, and one's alienated enjoyment of these greedy and foolish characters masks how being entrepreneurial is increasingly a feature of daily working life, as managers impress upon workers the need to become more productive and develop their human capital for the organisation. But if financial capital's power is now dependent on life itself to be economically productive and consent to its processes, then life itself – you and I – possess the democratic potential to say no, to draw on the negative and think and behave in entirely foreign ways to neoliberal capital.

Debt is both a means of control of the individual's time and possibilities, and an exciting vulnerability within financial capitalism. The processes of neoliberalism have led to a negation of wealth into abstracted finance, the production of goods into services, politics into marketing, social relations into economic relations, and time into debt. Negative capitalism facilitates this increasingly sped-up capitalism through a negation of time into an endless present, a flattening of disciplinary space so that work, socialising, pornography and shopping increasingly happen in one universal location, often the small black screens on our walls or in our very hands, whilst the political agency and economic rights of the worker are increasingly negated. Being in perpetual debt means that one's time spent not being productive is costly: how much interest has accumulated in this time on my debts? How much longer must I now work to catch up? Negative capitalism sustains itself through debt which in turn invests and colonises all future earnings, which are plunged into debt repayments, leading to new increasing symptoms of anxiety and depression in the UK. This anxiety is then manipulated by concerns over 'security' to generate new control architectures of surveillance and databases across the UK. But until now there has been no cohesive suggestion of a mass debt-strike. Rather than ever being vulnerable to the increasing interest rates of creditors and the increasing enclosure of public property by the markets, what if all those indebted were to strike back by refusing the only thing capital might need of them, debt?

A 'man is no longer a man confined but a man in debt': so Deleuze remarks in his "Postscript on Control Societies".[85] The exercise of neoliberal theory into practice has largely been determined by debt, where after reaching the status of influential idea it was parachuted into the debt crises of New York City (1976), the United Kingdom (1978-9), Latin America (1982) and others. Neoliberalisation is a process that transforms all social and political relations into economic relations, conforming with Deleuze's notion of the individual abstracted into a 'dividual', void of social content except economically-useful data.[86] Data is information, the basis of its own 'information economy', in effect a commodity – and when money is abstracted into financial capital, wage becomes a form of credit that workers sell in order to sustain present spending. By getting into debt, and in effect becoming credit commodities bought and sold by larger credit magnates – the worker becomes abstracted of future potential, their future time sold for a payment, that is, the debt to be repaid. Debt is paradigmatic of neoliberal control, the chief means by which subjects – be they individuals, businesses, or sovereign states – become subordinated and intrinsically controlled. Debt becomes an enclosure of the commons, what Steven Shaviro describes as a colonisation of the future, as individuals can no longer study, shop or afford to live in many urban areas without recourse to loans or credit cards.[87]

Debt on a mass scale has sustained and made possible the neoliberal project. In the UK, neoliberalism has been largely premised on huge national borrowing and a deregulation of credit controls, flooding the market consumers with cheap credit which has largely supplemented stagnating real wages and increasing poverty during this time.[88] As Marazzi argues, the servicing of debt has been a major commodity and source of disproportionate capital accumulation over the neoliberal era.[89] Post-Fordist financial capitalism has been presented with a problem of how to continue economic growth and production without producing further goods, resulting in what Deleuze calls a 'metaproduction' of financial speculation.[90] Marazzi's research finds that economic growth over the last twenty years has been based on a manipulation of mortgage loans and re-mortgaging, effectively allowing home-owners access to cheaper and cheaper credit.[91] Post-Fordist growth has therefore become based on 'non-wage incomes', a somewhat euphemistic reference to debt, whereby losses are socialised (national debt, austerity) and benefits are privatised (bankers' bonuses, MPs expenses, unpaid taxes).[92] Ultimately Western economies become ensnared in this speculative logic of borrowing and debt, where the powerful have a vested interest in maintaining the continued financialisation of everyday life by capital mechanisms. Public services are privatised; welfare-users and school-children become customers; whilst the final marks of citizenship (public service, safety) are replaced by CCTV and advertisements, the final form of civic information.

Debt also sustains and, in a very limited and problematic way, empowers many to participate in a consumer economy that would otherwise exclude the impoverished. Being in debt or depending on overdrafts and credit have become entirely normal in working-class and middle-class British life, but why has no-one stopped to ask what debt means? If it's a sacrifice of the future to sustain the present, why does one need to replace one debt with another on a regular basis? What was the original source of crisis that required one to sell one's future labour for credit in today's currency, and was this crisis fair, or were each of us taken advantage of? Ivor Southwood describes how debt is the closest thing to a collective identity the British people have, aside from a fear of terrorism.[93] What if the collectivity of indebted British workers were not dupes of persuasive credit card schemes, but forced into debt by unfair economic circumstances which rightly need to be rectified? Beyond individual debt, this language of debt and the necessity for cuts has become a new ideology: the national debt is now used to justify political and economic restructuring in language of 'sacrifice'. David Graeber has noted that much of the US debt is in fact owed to the Federal Reserve, effectively itself – interestingly the Federal Reserve was the engine of neoliberalism in the United States under Volcker.[94] Shaviro too argues that the 'free market' indeed forces us to be 'free': to cooperate in its price system as rational, efficient, "dynamic" individuals – a freedom which is increasingly based on credit to afford education, housing and consumer items.[95] This creates another experience of time beyond that of sheer instantaneity: the time of debt is one that extends into the future, speculating its own value that 'ravages the present in the name of a future that will never actually arrive; and it depletes our hopes for, and imaginings of, the future by turning it into nothing but a projection and endless repetition of the present'.[96] Debt has individually and socially become the pretext for further intrusions, demanding ever further sacrifices, for debts which no-one is ever realistically expected to repay, but must strive to do so all the same.

Private debt links the contemporary neoliberal worker with the citizen of the earlier democracies: it allows us to purchase what was once common and accessible by 'social rent' – decent housing, basic appliances and media devices, some kind of full-time employment.[97] Sean O'Connell's historical research into debt in working-class British communities found it to be a regular feature of working-class life long before the credit card. Working-class households, often led by women, have negotiated debt first with credit drapers, then mail-order catalogues, and now via the boom in doorstep moneylending since the 1980s onwards, as many became 'credit orphans' following increasing credit rating exclusions and deregulation.[98] The 'personal finance industry' and the no-win-no-fee insurance industries dominate television advertising during daytime hours when largely those unemployed, ill or caring for children will be watching TV, offering cheap loans, or advertising shops like Cash Converters or Bright House which have increasingly replaced the pawn-shop (and whose online store locator maps offer a topography of national poverty).[99] Perhaps the difference here is the recent phenomenon of both middle-class debt and national debt.

In a sense, neoliberalism was always predicated on a cheap trick, underscored by military power: allow workers to maintain living standards via cheap credit whilst wages in real-terms fall. As Graeber notes, money has always been something that never specifically existed, but has been a historical relation between banks and states seeking to pay for war.[100] The decision by US President Richard Nixon to end the fixed convertibility of gold to

US Dollars on 15 August 1971, terminating the global Bretton Woods agreement, was forced in order to continue the hugely expensive Indochina wars. The postwar Keynesian consensus had guaranteed full employment, expanding public services and inclusive education on the unwritten 'agreement' that workers would continue increasing productivity, accede to modernising labour practices, and that unions would regulate workforces to manage discipline. The collapse of this Fordist consensus is marked here: when productivity stagnates, Western economic hegemony is challenged. Post-Fordist financial credit, premised on debt, was a breakthrough that living standards could temporarily be maintained or frozen, through access to cheap credit – buy now and pay later become the policy of both individuals and national governments, a temporary political quick-fix at the time to guarantee backing from powerful capitalists in exchange for tax breaks. Margaret Thatcher's premiership demonstrates this in two ways: the support of the wealthy was assured immediately upon being elected in 1979, when she cut the personal income tax rate from 83% to 60%, whilst nearly doubling VAT from 8% to 15%, and cutting social spending; whilst she was able to temporarily buy public support through the sale of council houses to owners in the UK during the 1980s.[101] Obtaining credit was essential to continue purchasing basic items as prices rapidly rose through increased inflation and VAT. Thirty years on, decades of underfunded infrastructure is visible in the rotten, negated state of individuals, schools, housing, healthcare and communities. War becomes a powerful way of asserting Western hegemony whilst managing domestic unrest at home, with Pasquinelli arguing that it 'has a distinctly cathartic role for the *libido of a nation*'.[102] Thatcher's deregulation of credit controls in the 1980s gave new access to credit, and a short-term income was generated for many in buying and then subsequently selling (or sub-letting) council flats, but it took the controversial Falklands-Malvinas war of 1982 to establish real political support for Thatcher during a period of shrinking wages, rising inflation and unemployment, and overall social decline.[103]

A new economic and political identity was forged in the neoliberal era: 'Thatcherism' and 'Reaganism' converged on a right-wing religious morality of restrictive family values alongside neoliberal free markets. Corporations were free whilst individuals and trade unions became heavily restricted and regulated. The current effects of the neoliberal project demand that less employed workers work for longer hours, resulting in increasing productivity as before but with far cheaper and more disempowered labour. The decline of the social state, unwilling but also unable to provide infrastructure due to declining tax revenues from the wealthy, and at the mercy inevitably of credit rating agencies (Fitch, Moody's, and Standard & Poor's have become the king-makers of contemporary global politics), suggests private financial interests and stakeholders may be demanded to assume political control, given their possession of economic and therefore social power already. The question is whether citizens will have the strategy to take responsibility for their own decisions. Will obesity, depression, war and alcohol/drug dependency prove effective contraception to a new social democratic movement that might destroy its own indebted servitude?

The manipulation of debt during the neoliberal era has offset future production to abortively sustain contemporary consumerism – an effective sale of future labour, the ultimate speculation and permeation of life by capital. This can be under-stood in the looming £191billion debt that students will owe by 2047, according to latest government estimates, a figure which has already risen from the £67billion estimate last year.[104] Find evidence of this in the increasing capital imbalance between capital-accumulating states (China, India, the oil-producing states) and capital-borrowing states (US, UK, Ireland and the southern Eurozone states), which has required these states to effectively guarantee through credit and bond-purchases the unsustainable consumerism and public expenditure of the citizens and governments of these indebted states.[105] In many ways debt has unnaturally allowed consumption and economic production in declining states, a temporary economic solution which defers bankruptcy or social collapse to an abandoned future – "when the shit hits the fan, we won't be in government".

Keynesianism has the capacity to redirect state expenditure into socially munificent projects but this required precisely the international Bretton Woods international banking agreement dissolved in 1971. National currencies no longer have the power or ability to protect themselves against central banks and credit markets, and it is only military power that confirms the UK and the US as independent and powerful forces when their own currencies and economies are in such indebted, deregulated and hence uncontrollable disarray. Global financial exchange is underscored by nothing except the abstract debts of its workers, an abstract debt which would be fictitious were it not brutally underscored by bailiffs, police forces and national military machines. Thus debt has sustained impossible levels of consumption in declining states, a temporary economic solution which defers bankruptcy and social collapse to some unknown point in an increasingly unlikely and ruined future.

Despite various attempts at economic stimulus since 2008, the global debt crisis is again flaring up in the collapse of the Eurozone and further collapse of American currency markets, with rounds of 'quantitative easing' compounding the fact that money is now largely fictional, speculative and based on no value apart from the hegemonic power of those who issue it. At this stage, the only option for most western economies is to go into further sovereign debt (by selling bonds), whilst encouraging consumers to do the same. Whilst China may be behind many of the loans, negative capitalism has no responsible sovereign. The terrifying spectre haunting the neoliberal era is universal debt, with no obvious creditor, and no possible means of ever repaying a debt owed. The more literary readings of Marx's works have attended to his metaphors of spectres, vampires, and the undead in his descriptions of capital.[106] Another spectre looming behind this is perhaps 'zombie banks', inflated by state capital to continue appearing as functioning, lending banks when in fact their activities or independence have long been nil, another iconic contradiction of the neoliberal era.[107]

Is capital itself undead, one that has deferred its imminent organic death by structural contradiction by a Frankenstein-like appearance of life as debt? Perhaps it is not capital which is undead, but workers, 'life', neither alive nor dead but abstracted, negated and organised into financial streams which are used to afford a decreasingly minimal basic biopolitical support – precarious labour, declining infrastructure, reduction of agency to forged consent, reduction of public spaces to privatised control. Negative capitalism abstracts all labour-relations into debt-creditor relations, where most workers are entirely disempowered and limited by their debts to maintain membership and complicity in a system of capitalist accumulation which they gain no real benefit from, and which many cynically admit is a rigged show. To compound the Kafkaesque 'indefinite postponement', there is increasingly no possibility for many nation-states of becoming bankrupt either.[108] Perhaps only a campaign of systematic mass-bankruptcies and hacking into financial systems and currency markets will effect some kind of redress of this negation of future and labour-in-potential by debt.

5

Anxiety Machines

The accounts of sociologists, philosophers, and economists of the last forty years often repeat the same riffs of 'ephemerality, fragmentation, chaos' to describe the neoliberal era as beyond modernity, in a state of arrested postmodernity.[109] For a period marked by uncertainty and a certain non-status (from post to where?), it is curious that Charles Baudelaire once again becomes the prophet and poet of this 'instantaneity' and 'time-space compression', to employ two influential terms of our era from Jameson and Harvey.[110] Capitalist speeds from the 19th century workhouse through to the 20th century industrialised killing fields of the world wars have been repeatedly marked by anxiety and hysteria. Anxiety and fear are no doubt psychological marks of domination in all social structures, but a specific anxiety and fear emerges in financial capitalism by the increasing speeds and pressures of working and living in the neoliberal era. This is facilitated by new information technologies such as the home PC, the Internet, the hand-held network device, and finally the social networking sites. Castells and Deleuze both converge in describing our culture as shifting from the 'actual' to the 'virtual', but the virtual itself only explains how culture is present in *digitised* information.[111] Digitisation itself is the fundamental shift of the contemporary era, the environment where new cultural forms are rapidly coming into being. It occurs in the transformation of content from specific, analogue formats to encoded digital information – the film-reel, the painting, the book, and the piano solo are replaced by the polished-up and perfected .mp4, .jpeg, .pdf, .docx and .mp3. Benjamin described in the earlier part of the 20th century the dangers of the technical reproduction of images in terms of a lost aura and experience; I want to advance beyond this that neoliberal capitalism must be understood by its specific technologies of reproducible, digitisable information; and that this negation and abstraction of all phenomena into digitised data formats has contributed to an increasing collective anxiety.[112]

Bifo too observes that this collective panic is compounded by the excessive onslaught of information that explodes from media interfaces and overwhelms one's neurones.[113] Work and social lives increasingly demand hand-held phone devices that negate time and space constraints to link workers into immaterial networks of reaction with immediacy. Whilst the major sociologists of neoliberal modernity like Castells have noted the significant global increase of mobile phones and Internet access, an August 2011 Ofcom report finds that 47% of teenagers surveyed owned a smartphone, and of these, 60% felt 'addicted' (the report also notes a general decline in TV and reading activities at the expense of smartphone communications connectivity).[114] Such technologies do not dissolve the disciplines but extend their influence further: the modern dividual must work harder, longer, and with far more distraction in what Virilio calls a 'tele-present' world, a daily interaction increasingly dependent on networks.[115] Consider the panic of losing a mobile phone at home now, or the leisure of not checking and responding to emails over a 24-hour period.

The experience of social space has shifted from tangible locations (clubs, bars, halls, and so on) to immaterial social networks; a shift to immateriality that reflects the declining funding and use of public spaces, which have either closed or become enclosed by security architectures. As well as this negation of space, time too has been negated by increasing speeds of information flows, a shift to what Castells terms 'timeless time'.[116] Castells astutely details how biological time is negated by the choice to have children far later in life via IVF treatments; how social time, working-time, or family time is negated by the flexible nature of working, which too can be now done at home, and at all hours.[117] Knowledge and news depreciate at an increasing rate: new content is constantly demanded just-in-time, causing time itself to flatten. As economist Enzo Rullani puts it, 'All the actors of knowledge economy are engaged in a *race against time*, where running is necessary simply to maintain the same position and not fall behind'.[118] Time diminishes as the space of work, family, shopping, pornography and social interaction interweave into one flattened, expanded universal space, now located on a screen or hand-held media device.

These shifts occur at the moment when the public sector and the public space disappear into private ownership. Richard Sennett documented the beginning of this trend back in 1974. For him, 'public space is an area to move through, not be in...a derivative of movement'.[119] Yet whilst Sennett's anxieties of a city governed around speed and movement focuses on the car, it is an entirely immaterial kind of flow, that of money, detached from the gold standard, passing trading floors in seconds without regulation, that accelerates and undoes the public. As infrastructure, healthcare, housing and entire state finances become privatised and sold to international financiers or rival states, the city of motion signals a dangerous vulnerability. But Sennett provides another equally worrying thought about the loss of public space:

> When everyone has each other under surveillance, sociability decreases, silence being the only form of protection...Human beings need to have some distance from intimate observation by others in order to feel sociable.[120]

Whilst Sennett has in mind the open-plan office, another feature of flexible precarious labour organisation, it reminds one of the far more insidious surveillance of the public space via CCTV, and of the private space via the extensive records kept of one's phone-calls, emails and movements .For Paul Virilio too, the very spatiality of the city itself has unravelled via the increased speeds of information, and the collapse of separate spaces where different activities might occur. The city is no longer a 'space' in any sense – it is a labyrinth of 'interfaces' and screens: 'the way one gains access to the city is no longer through a gate, an arch of triumph, but rather through an electronic audiencing system'.121 Work is intensified into continual timeless activity, debt is universal, and connectivity must be continuous.

Tim Berners-Lee, creator of fundamental Internet protocols like html and the world wide web, describes his vision of total connectivity – 'anything being potentially connected with anything' – where machines, information systems and bodies become fused into one organic-biopolitical network that 'brings the workings of society closer to the workings of our minds'.122 Media, financial and medical networks coil together in the commercial motives of their billionaire owners and service providers to permeate all social life with a protocological 'topology of control' and regulation of life, forged consent and labour control – a field of power relations like that encountered earlier in Foucault.123 These arrangements of networks can be conceived in terms of symmetry, whereby the weight of capital distorts and transforms the network space around it, perhaps like how black holes distort the gravity of space and light around them in their rapacious dark energy.124 This might be the ultimate diagram of negative capitalism: as Galloway and Thacker tell us, 'In contemporary biopolitics, the body is a database, and informatics is the search engine'.125 The vast bureaucracy of the Castle is now paperless, mediated through horizontal (yet still hierarchical) networks of power, and the price of this control is an increasingly psychologically-internalised waste-heap of workers' anxiety.

The *Diagnostic and Statistical Manual of Mental Disorders* (DSM) of the American Psychiatric Association is frequently drawn on as the gospel-truth of all mental health disorders, with commentators repeatedly citing the arrival of *DSM III* in 1980 as a 'scientific revolution', codifying mental disorder within a new system of scientific management.[126] Its most recent 2004 IV-TR edition describes 'Generalized Anxiety Disorder' as 'excessive anxiety and worry', an uncontrollable worry that largely dominates the sufferer's time, and usually defined by three or more symptoms, including 'restlessness, being easily fatigued, difficulty concentrating, irritability, muscle tension, and disturbed sleep'.[127] These symptoms describe those of the precarious worker, exhausted, fed up, tired yet compelled to stay awake just to finish a little more work from home, a microwave-meal usually spilt over their laptop. Depression and exhaustion are endemic, and act as marks of an affective and immaterial economy where employment is now to be found in the services – retail, leisure, call-centres, cleaning, childcare, sex work – where an inflated mood, one indeed of motivation, is required. I can only smile for a certain amount of time before my jaw aches. Individuality becomes another part of the service worker's uniform. There's a raft of recent reports detailing increasing levels of depression and anxiety: a 2003 survey by the American Medical Association (AMA) found that 10% of 15-54 year olds surveyed had had an episode of 'major depression' in the last 12 months, with 17% of these in their lifetime; a figure echoing the 15.1% found to be suffering from 'common mental disorders' (stress, anxiety and depression) by the NHS's 2007 adult survey.[128] Furthermore women were found to be twice as likely to suffer from depression as men on average both in the AMA and NHS Surveys – the 15.1% average comes from 12.5% in men, 19.7% in women.[129] The NHS Survey also found that self-harm and suicidal behaviours in women had increased since 2000, with 'being female' at one point listed by the survey as a source of depression, without irony or sociological comment.[130]

Given the general, non-personal causes of these common mental disorders (work stress, social isolation, inadequate housing, debt, alcohol and substance misuse), there is clear evidence beyond the obvious observations of one's surroundings that overall quality of life is declining during the neoliberal era, a decline that has affected men and women in different ways, with a high suicide rate amongst men on the one hand, as seen earlier, and a higher incidence of depression among women on the other.[131] Recent employment statistics demonstrate that woman have been adversely affected by the large redundancies within the public services in the UK following the neoliberal austerity cuts, with a March 2011 TUC report finding female unemployment had risen 0.5 points to its highest level since 1988.[132] Single-parent families are largely led by females, who are struggling with reducing welfare support, inflation and reduced employment opportunities, all the while continually demonised by the right-wing media and Conservative governments as 'feckless' and irresponsible.[133] Austerity becomes the 'state of exception' of British neoliberalism, with the need for deficit cuts being used both by Thatcher, Brown and now Cameron to further reduce welfare and support services whilst justifying wage freezes and unemployment, which adversely affect women.[134] The indicative phenomenon of eating disorders in women during the neoliberal era have generally increased, at least in terms of popular reflection and discussion.[135] I want to resist making both the traditional 'cultural dupe' fallacy of Theodor Adorno whilst rejecting the passive liberal 'oppositional strategies' of Stuart Hall, by arguing that eating disorders tell us about control.[136] Eating disorders are largely thought to occur in women and men as the sufferer struggles to assert control over one part of their own lives – their calorie consumption and exercise – usually in order to compensate for a wider lack of control in their psychosocial lives. The eating disorder may well be exacerbated by the wider existential insecurity of negative capitalism, a precarity that generally affects women more than men, and the young more than the old.

Reports in April 2011 balefully announced that antide-pressant prescriptions had risen by 43% over the past five years, with London health authorities alone spending £20million annually on anti-depressant medication.[137] Although there are numerous problems with the reliability of statistics concerning actual depression amongst the population, the development and normalisation of psychopharmacological treatments is signif-icant. Indeed reports in 2004 suggested that traces of Prozac itself had been discovered in London's water supply, perhaps the ultimate perfection of biopolitical management.[138] Carl Walker draws attention to World Health Organisation predictions that by 2020 depressive disorders will be the leading cause of disability and disease burden across the globe.[139] Walker finds a poor material standard of living accounting for nearly 25% of cases of common mental disorder in 1998, a figure which given increasing poverty, debt and social inequality will have risen.[140]

Psychiatry is doubly insightful in terms of neoliberalism and control societies: for a start, the psychiatric clinic is one of pioneering sites of discipline for Foucault, sites which Deleuze argued were now in decline.[141] Education facilities, prisons, factories, hospitals and psychiatric hospitals have all fallen into stagnation and decline in the US and UK during the neoliberal era, primarily due to a decline in government funding or, specif-ically in the UK, a diversion of public funding into Private Finance Initiative schemes and into the hands of private companies and consultancy firms. The family, another site of discipline, has also effectively declined from the 1980s due to increasing rates of divorce, whilst deindustrialisation and a freeze in the construction of housing and infrastructure (until a thaw during the New Labour government) has seen a continuous real decline in what Foucault described as disciplinary institu-tions.[142] This could present a crisis of biopolitics given that the facilities for managing life are diminishing. Yet negative capitalism offers a perfection of the regulation of life – the workplace, psychiatric treatment, and the university are now open at all hours – one can work or receive advice from a range of choices online, whilst personal technologies enable one to participate in these networks at all hours. The psychiatric hospital specifically declined due to a mixture of decreasing infrastructure expenditure and the wider effects of the anti-psychiatry campaign from the mid-1960s, which presented the public and policy-makers with grotesque images of institutional-isation, its moralistic or arbitrary labelling of conditions, and exaggerations of the dangers of Electro-Convulsive Therapy.[143] New 'Care in the Community' schemes initiated by Enoch Powell onwards could only be facilitated by the mass-development of psychopharmacology, the treatment of psychiatric disorders through drug therapies. As a fledgling arena of research, a huge spate of publications on psychopharmacology began from the mid-1970s and appeared throughout the 1980s, during which the fairly universal treatment of psychological disorders by drugs was established.[144]

Psychopharmacology assumes that psychiatric disorders are malfunctions of neuronal chemistry which can, through the correct rational application of scientific intervention, be univer-sally treated or managed. The onus is on both an infallible scien-tific method and the individual to conform and adhere to treatment. Disorders are therefore caused by the individual and not the circumstances or psychosocial conflicts around them, as psychoanalysis had previously contested. In such a manner, neoliberal control permeates the entire 'sick' body: the discipline of visiting the therapist or the site of the clinic is replaced with the continuous intervention of chemicals. The individual is now free to challenge and overcome their problems, through a mixture of prescribed treatment and usually through the additional cognitive re-programming of more positive mindsets.

Psychopharmacology demonstrates the entire workings of neoliberalism in one section of society through a curious hegemonic transformation: the postwar consensus of Keynesianism and social democracy, Fordism and psychoanalysis with it, are all marked with a social engagement with problems. This is a social politic, one that addressed and engaged with problems of deviance, health, upbringing, employment and poverty. Although it was in some ways a superficial consensus that sought to prevent the onset of Communism in Western Europe and the US, as critics like Graeber have pointed, it was a politic that emphasised the benefit and use of society to manage life and treat problems.[145] The shift to post-Fordism, neoliberalism and psychopharmacology represents a shift to an economic politic, where disorder is managed by a mixture of mathematical-scientific reasoning, be it the market or the technological management of illness, where 'unproductive' industries are outsourced and labour abstracted.

Benjamin Franklin, a key architect in the formation of the modern American state, once said that 'God helps them who help themselves'.[146] Franklin's moral justification for private property demonstrates that the neoliberal faith in divinely-ordained capitalism is old. Whilst Thatcher and Reagan preached a mutilated version of the Bible during the 1980s, neoliberal bankers preached a Darwin-lite survival of the fittest narrative (think of the drear image of yuppies quoting Sun Tzu or Herbert Spencer), a narrative that legitimised their own power as a reflection of natural strength. The difference in the contemporary neoliberal era is the lack of counter-narrative: this is what is meant by contemporaries who angst over the lack of an organised (traditional-looking) Left-wing movement in the West, or who bemoan the loss of the 'future'. One counter-narrative for anxiety machines might be: wealth is unduly taken, work is a burden if not done out of choice, that expecting work to deliver a sense of purpose, identity and friendships is absurd.

Undeniable, but the marks of an unhappy and negated life. Work itself is the point of control, generating an internal self-management of time, with materialism its measure and anxiety its soundtrack. Bound in captivity to an unfortunate situation one cannot escape, the common psychological reaction is to identity with the interests of the captor, find hope and justification in negative circumstances: the workaholic, Stockholm Syndrome and the Voltaire's character Pangloss with his argument, faced with the best of 18th century misery that this is "the best of all possible worlds", converges. Workers become the most sincere defenders of their own austerity cuts, a necessary and temporary prick like all those others before, whilst bankers and traders use the cover of crisis to accumulate more capital and increase their share of the collective wealth.

Work is a serious problem for any political account of the contemporary. There is no escape from work: labour and the production of food and goods are necessary to creating and maintaining stable societies. Although working lives are becoming more precarious in the West, they pale in comparison to factory conditions say in 1850 Britain, where various Factory Acts such as that of 1833, which sought to limit the working day of children under 13 to no more than 9 hours a day, or 48 hours a week; or the 1847 Factory Act, which compassionately restricted the working day for young people and women to just ten hours a day.[147] The despair of the bored modern office worker seems pathetic in comparison. Workers were paid by the day rather than the hour, hence the desire for factory-owners to have them working for as long as possible. The introduction of the wage relation was a major political gain from the industrial serfdom that preceded it. The factory system reminds us that discussion of info-capitalism is also redundant: the textile and data-chip factories exist in even greater numbers, only in parts of the world out of sight of labour regulation. Although poverty is real and not simply 'relative', at least not in my experiences working with vulnerable people and growing up in London, access to luxury goods has become much cheaper in recent years. The fear of both Karl Marx and Oscar Wilde that the eventual perfection of capitalism would lead to the disappearance, and hence mass starvation, of labour remains unfounded: capital always needs to maintain demand.[148] The cheap electronic luxury is a right and mark of citizenship in the current consumer covenant: capital provides us with access to consumption, and public information appeals to us as consumers and little more. Further, rather than advanced production now guaranteeing each of us a life of deserved leisure as envisioned by the modernist utopias of the early 20th century, the factory and mine have been replaced by the mall and call-centre: whatever happens, each of us must work, no matter how utterly superfluous the vocation. Work itself is the science of managing populations. What would happen if everyone refused to work for the week?

Working and consuming therefore go arm-in-arm in this new neoliberal citizenship. As workers drive themselves harder for longer hours in either stressful or dull vocations, the only form of public information – advertisements – bombard workers with dreamy products that generate an insatiable hunger for new goods and services. In *The Philosophy of Money* (1900), Georg Simmel noted that the significance of the money relation was to establish an impersonal and symbolic relation of the human 'self' with the world, increasingly mediated through a system of objects or commodities. "I buy this, this is who I am" is a statement effectively marketed by Coca-Cola and visible in the shelves of any modern flat, where people define themselves by the books, video-games, films, music collections, artwork, clothes or perfume they have bought. Satisfying these needs is stressful: people feel inadequate about their appearance or more basic existence, and the pressure of work and unrealistic expectations of being happy for its own sake often cause personal relationships to break down. Consumption becomes the consistent basis of modern identity.

Perhaps the more fundamental weakness is the preoccupation with happiness, of individual happiness for its own sake. Happiness is something one feels entitled to – its lack, rather than specific causes for suffering, lead to a general middle-class unhappiness, known since Charles Baudelaire as ennui. But the danger of seeking happiness or self-fulfilment for its own sake is its implied negation: boredom and collective identity. A life spent escaping boredom involves quitting jobs, relationships, allowing that boredom to manage and determine one's life. It is an infantile fear of death and responsibility, and one founded on an equally infantile narcissism – "I alone have the right to be happy, and my desires must always come first, for I am the most important". Infantilisation is another hallmark of negative capitalism, as is the neurotic protection of the individual, which like in any Kafka novel is inevitably bound to alienation and frustrated desire. One's expectations for continual stimulation and new objects automatically lead to dissatisfaction and restlessness that work and further consumption alone can allay – a little more retail therapy. Ironically, the middle-class hippies of the 1960s largely got what they wanted: politicians today talk about 'freedom' and fight 'just' wars; corporate management now celebrates 'individuality' and 'creativity'. The anti-chav backlash reflects a middle-class insecurity with threatened status. The search for individual happiness itself is part of the drug of contemporary cynicism. Cooperation and coming together in democratic communities to realise one's development collectively, rather than as sad individuals, offers one solution.

Life without work is a naïve aspiration: instead, one must learn how to redefine one's identity beyond work. Collectively, full employment with reduced working hours for all would be one effective division of labour that could both develop and maintain a domestic industrialised manufacture of goods, and provide social access to work. The task of a different education system could then be not just the production of good workers or God-fearers but citizens who are creative, self-sufficient and democratically-minded, ones who can define their lives by their relationships, skills, creative interests and quality of conversation. More realistically, a political movement around work could call for improved protections for labour both nationally and globally – the introduction of a global and universal living wage via a global universal currency, a legal universal restriction on working hours, a serious advance in equal opportunities (essential when one recalls the pay gap between men or women, or the lack of ethnic minority or working-class professionals in public life), and the scrutiny and punishment of corporations who directly or indirectly damage workers and ecosystems, through exposure to toxic materials, poor provision of safety procedures, and so on.

Stable employment in the contemporary neoliberal era has effectively become non-existent, as control is manifested through absolute precarity and flexibility of workers, easily dismissed and lacking roots to establish solidarity with other workers. All labour becomes part-time, casualised and insecure, reflected in the 2011 CIPD Employment barometer, predicting correctly for 2011 that the majority of new jobs created would be temporary, part-time, casual and entirely lacking in security.[149] Recalling Foucault's discussion of the Panopticon in Chapter Two, Bentham's principles of controlling the mind, rather than just the body of the worker, are the hallmarks of control societies, and these features are clearly identifiable in the anxiety and management of the modern workplace. As Bentham's proposed system for managing prisoners put it back in 1787, it offered a 'new mode of obtaining power of mind over mind, in a quantity hitherto without example'.[150] Work is the site of increasingly intensive management: Bentham's panoptical principles have been put into place by surveillance computer programmes that restrict email access, by employers who check their workers'

Facebook pages, and within an open-plan office where every behaviour is on scrutiny and workers are compelled to remain productive and smiley-faced without a private space to slack or curse their managers or colleagues. Such surveillance does not simply monitor for misdemeanours: it also limits the worker's capacity to speak out or act independently for fear of future retribution, rendering she/he infantile, without choice and anxiously dreading exposure.

These contemporary features of modern workplace management have their roots in the industrialised 'science' of management introduced by F.W. Taylor in 1911, a science that explicitly calls for the negation of workers' intelligence into careful management. Taylor envisioned managers 'gathering together all of the traditional knowledge which in the past has been possessed by the workmen and then of classifying, tabulating, and reducing this knowledge to rules, laws, and formulae'.[151] Mark Fisher in *Capitalist Realism* coins the term 'market Stalinism' to describe the heavy and seemingly-pointless intervention of auditing in a British Further Education college, but his argument misses the more fundamental shift: intensive management and auditing have been effected in order to fully control the worker.[152] Auditing becomes like the military drill: a sign of conformity and obedience, introduced further and further into previously middle-class, creative and knowledge-based jobs. It is also a marker of the proletarianisation of these jobs – cuts in real wages and pensions are matched by further intervention in the daily tasks of the worker. Fear compels the worker to adhere to this intensive intervention of management.

This language of fear is in turn taken up by those in power. Recently Oliver Letwin, Policy Minister for the current Coalition government, declared that public sector workers needed more 'fear' in order to work effectively and appropriately compete with the societal demands made of them.[153] Anxiety – a state of dread of an unknown object – would be more appropriate. Whilst precarity and debt are regular features of often casualised working-class life and labour, the novelty of neoliberalism is its proletarianisation of the middle class in order to maintain increasing capital accumulation for the very wealthy. Hence a 2011 Institute for Fiscal Studies report found that whilst incomes generally rose during the New Labour governments (by about 1.9% annually from 1997-2010), income inequality as measured by the Gini co-efficient also markedly rose to 0.36 in 2007-8, the highest level since the 1940s and well above the marked rise of 0.25 in 1979 under Thatcher.[154] Given that New Labour saw relative poverty fall during its government, this inequality was generated by the vastly increasing earnings at the very top 0.1% of earners, with poverty largely alleviated by increased benefits and tax credits under Labour, which are now being reduced and in many cases removed by the current Coalition government.[155]

Curiously there is a growing class anger and defensiveness in the British middle-class Right-wing, in authors and journalists like Peter Oborne, John Gray, J.G. Ballard, and Peter Wilby. As informational labour is off-shored to cheaper labour sites in China and India, there will be a collapse in the living standards of the Western middle-classes. And with shrinking state expenditure on welfare, it is not unreasonable to predict that absolute poverty and destitution will become even more common than they already are. Hence recent years have been marked by the prospect of middle-class revolt, as politically disenfranchised middle-class youth with no clear stake in the comfortable exploitation of the poor begin to get angry, whilst the working class and underclass, disenfranchised for longer and therefore more cynical about alternatives, become even more desperate. Whether this will lead to anything other than right-wing brute fascism or left-wing elitist melancholia of comparable periods in the 20th century remains to be seen.

Such controls actuate a greater security and control under the rubric of freedom, in the same manner that Western-led global warfare has, if anything, increased during the neoliberal era but under the precise, economic rationale of smart-bombs and drone attacks. As Lewis puts it, 'the personal is not political; the personal is biological', and beneath statistics there is an increasingly high provision of antidepressants to those groups marginalised by patriarchal neoliberal capitalism – women, the unemployed, working-class urban youth, ethnic minorities, immigrants.[156] One-fifth of all working days in Britain are estimated as lost due to anxiety and depression forcing workers to take time off, a very shaky estimate given the stigma and perceived weakness of openly telling managers of mental health problems; but given the current prospect of increasing working hours in Britain as labour regulations are further 'liberalised', this anxiety will only continue.[157] Freud tells us that whilst fear regards a specific object, anxiety is an indefinite state without object, which seeks to alert us of an 'unknown' danger one is ignorant of and vulnerable to.[158] Anxiety is the condition of the disempowered, and Freud notes how it is only by becoming aware of the repressed fear-object (castration, fear of temptation) that one can overcome the anxious state.[159]

Although many workers are well aware what it is which causes their anxiety and debt in the short-term, perhaps the time comes now for a collective therapeutic catharsis of the neurosis-anxiety of negative capitalism, and its continuous controlling demands for productivity. Such a catharsis might begin with a violent libidinal overthrow, rejecting stoical acceptances of continual deprivation, and for once taking responsibility of winning and attaining democratic desire. This means acting up, and not expecting events like 'the end of the world' or other hopeful catastrophes to come and break clean with a ritual holocaust. It requires politically claiming feelings like humour, immorality and anger instead of suspect old tripe like righteousness or dignity. It demands new behaviours like hacking, mobbing, debt-strikes and non-working. As a democratic body, rather than an idiotic swarm of smartphone-bashing individuals, the focus is the destruction and transformation of the outside – financial capital, ignorance, fascism, militarism – rather than angsty debates of 'who we are' and good-intentioned identity politics that render the contemporary resistance to financial capitalism safely irrelevant and impotent. It requires ultimately a political reclamation of negativity.

The negative is the space of creative difference, out of which madness, gambling one's life in spite bad odds, chaos and the night of the *Walpurgisnacht* of Goethe or lairy nocturnal partying all emerge, out of poetry, blackness, sex, out of deep bass and physical touch. The space of consensus, goodness and cynicism is positive, it faces the negative and composes an excuse, a reactionary response which is the positive, the idiot plaster of affirmation. Optimism cannot just mean cobbling together convenient lies to make unhappy people more able to face their misfortunes, but instead contains the creativity to sidestep all existing meanings and engage on an entirely new and unknown path or activity. Optimism is creative, and therefore draws on the negative. Pessimism is reactionary, and therefore is forced to assemble a positive. Its failure to confront the violent nature of desire in life, both cultural and biological, forces it into cynical submission to forces more willing to creatively assert themselves. Neoliberalism is one such powerful system, and so this is ample time to pull together a new meaning and desire, out of the eternal minus of our own negativity.

Drawing on the negative does not mean simply being 'bad' or carrying out violent or criminal acts against other people: there are plenty of religious fools, fascist vigilantes and politicians happily able to carry out mass murder under the lie of some positive necessity. Instead negativity offers a creative and hedonistic subversion that corrupts codes of existing boring behaviour. Instead of town hall debates or steering committees for the coming revolution, negativity spells out new political acts like targeted looting, flashmobs at financial headquarters, a spontaneous rave at a toff wine reception – anything against alienation. Negativity embodies mass creative dissent, is the play of war within our chests, and is the nerve and charm that gets discussion going on public transport or at a local youth centre or disability peer-support group where all those willing agree to actually go and do something about expensive fares, or rents, or discrimination by cops or clerks, with cheeky cunning and maybe Dutch Courage, taking struggles out onto the streets where the actions of history most often play out. The task of a negative social democratic revolt is to demonstrate how history is transformed through spontaneous and devious eruptions of life. Humanity is not doomed by knowledge: expertise, technology and cunning are gifts that democratic communities can use to develop their own sites of production, whilst sabotaging any rival capital that operates under the irrational private profit motive. History will not be created by the nihilists, but by those who determine to leave behind their nihilistic contemporaries.

The modern individual is condemned to ignorance, to not getting what one wants, so long as one operates purely as an individual, as a customer. But this aloof resignation and cynicism is a boring psychological armour which sanctions things as they currently stand, in all their anxious and self-destructive order. Nothing is lost, and everything is still to play for: pleasure is release from anxiety. The time is ripe to abandon the cynicism and melancholia of the aloof and impotent individual, and venture into the dark pleasure of the negative, the powerful and pulsating substance of life, currently invested by capital, which might be moulded into a new democratic body, provided it can first learn how to speak.

6

Perverted by Language

Neoliberalism speaks a language of hysteria, where spasmodic and violent gestures, accompanied by a semantically meaningless and hyperactive language masks a repressed anxiety. Whilst a language of fear is used by neoliberal government leaders to pressure workers to become even more 'competitive', what other instances of anxiety disorders are being wilfully fomented by control architectures? A concern with increasing control was marked by the 2006 Information Commissioner's announcement that Britain was 'sleepwalking into a surveillance state'.[160] The use of CCTV has markedly risen in the UK since 1993 following its success in catching the young killers of toddler Jamie Bulger, which generated a moral panic at the time over the apparent corruption of children and the need for urgent moral policing.[161] Reliable nationwide statistics do not exist for the total CCTV usage, but until1998 an average of 75% of the Home Office's Crime Prevention Budget was spent on CCTV systems (£8.5m), with a further £170m made available up until 2003.[162] Estimates vary between the highly flawed but oft-quoted number of 4.2 million (based on two south-west London streets in 2002!) and the more recent figure of 1.8 million, but local councils only keep records of their own CCTV usage, excluding private surveillance by individuals and business-owners.[163] Whatever the actual figure, the normalisation of surveillance is most significant, even where police and Home Office reports have denounced its efficacy.[164] As an architecture of control, CCTV has been remarkably successful: over 1,474 people have been charged in England following the August 2011 riots, much of the evidence largely combed by police officers from CCTV footage.[165] It has additionally operated with a preventative Panopticon effect: numerous surveys report a decline in burglaries and car theft in locations where CCTV is evident, despite many CCTV cameras being incorrectly installed, or produce footage that is unusable in court.[166] What is most fundamental about mass surveillance is not the validity of information gathered, but the social and psychological effect of being continually monitored.

CCTV is just one short-term strategy of local councils and business-owners to increase security without the expense of attempting to solve or engage in the deeper causes of crime and deviancy. Heather Brooke has used Freedom of Information requests to uncover how much information is being kept on individuals by the state on various databases. She was shocked to find that the then-Labour government had been spending £16 billion a year on IT projects largely establishing new databases, from the National DNA database to innumerable others monitoring children's development and predicting criminal behaviour, as well as lavishly expensive NHS databases.[167] Much of these database details were being lost by careless officials or commercially sold to private firms, yet a further £100 billion had (around 2009) been earmarked to fund further government IT schemes, mostly via the Private Finance Initiative under New Labour, which tendered public services to private profit-making corporations like Capita, which boasted a 30% success rate in meeting its contracts.[168] Despite the current Coalition government dismantling the DNA database, it continues to tender out other IT projects to private organisations, continuing the ongoing neoliberal project to develop a major immaterial control infrastructure, at a time when there is apparently insufficient money for new housing, current pension provision or maintained welfare support for the most vulnerable. Surveillance thereby occurs as the more blatant monitoring of public spaces through CCTV alongside monitoring of private details on these databases.

Both cases involve an increasing concern and anxiety over security – the safety of children, the concerns with violent street crime and youth violence – that is then used to justify establishing expensive apparatuses of control that permeate everyday life.[169] These technologies, used to monitor and control public life, are first introduced as strategies of crime prevention. Yet as Nick Davies finds, in a criminal justice system where 97% of criminal charges are dropped, and where no attempt is made to solve the alcohol, substance misuse or mental health problems that many prisoners suffer from, the only purpose surely is the policing of the ordinary law-abiding citizen, for whom alone this control system works well.[170] Individuals abandon some of their liberty and privacy in exchange for security. At the same time, a lack of investment and sustained challenge to the core causes of poverty and social disintegration – those which often lead to criminal behaviours and criminalisation in the first place – seemingly justifies further need for increasingly punitive and pervasive control. It is a vicious circle demonstrated by the August 2011 riots, which began in areas of high unemployment and poverty.[171] The move to criminal monitoring of public places, facilitated and in a sense funded by public anxieties over crime, acts as a privatisation of social space. Local councils establish their own databases and CCTV systems; at the same time, they become 'entrepreneurial' as Harvey put it, increasing control architectures whilst transferring social housing, services, deindustrialised land into private hands under the rubric of urban regeneration.[172] This is carried out usually with a plethora of inclusive language and sparky apolitical public art, as in the recent redevelopment of Stratford for the 2012 Olympics or in the earlier redevelopment of the London Docklands. Banishment of the poor and gentrification mark the perfection of biopolitical organisation, as previously subsistent or unproductive aspects of social life are colonised, destroyed and re-used, like the workings of the insect parasite Cordyceps, exciting property prices in the process.[173] Each worker too suffers the fate of Agamben's notion of the 'whatever being', a non-worker emptied of authenticity, emptied even of the status of labour, of worker, of man or woman – instead now abstracted into continuous productivity and control.[174]

Neoliberal techniques of control infantilise citizens into consumers. Laura Oldfield Ford has documented in her zine series *Savage Messiah* how processes of gentrification and infantilisation established a vicious fault-line of class war. Architecture becomes a cynical strategy of social management and expropriation, glimpsed in the contemporary urban street-scene where gentrification, marked by the construction of luxury gated communities or 'yuppiedromes', jostles with the infantilisation of the new civic buildings, modern social housing and the hopeless 'jobcentreplus' (PR-rebranding fail – jobcentre plus what, security guards?). This 'friendly architecture' is defined by a perverse mixture of wavy roofs and mixed material cladding, security grilles, roving security guards and oversized colourful furniture: 'There's this playschool architecture everywhere, it acts as a frame and a decoy, as if in the '90s all battles were won'.[175] This infantilisation is the effect of decades of gradual social disempowerment through diminishing labour rights, declining real political agency, a privatisation of public infrastructure and healthcare, and a wider disappearance of public spaces through new security technologies, transforming public spaces into sites of suspicion and control.[176]

Paolo Virno uses Heidegger's description of fear to offer a notion of popular anguish and alienation as a collective 'not feeling at home', leading to a widespread metropolitan 'childishness'.[177] Virno is attempting an ontological description of alienation in total, but when deprivation of activity and agency is combined with a more practical inability to be at home because of longer and more unstructured working hours, a powerful process is at work: a fundamental disempowerment through alienation and a negation of workers' time, space, and mature ability to make independent decisions.[178] Home CCTV systems have been sold by security companies and are increasingly popular, whilst the public spread of CCTV was marked by a new televised form of entertainment, as drunks, criminals and even reality TV contestants amused and entertained record audience figures via their recorded CCTV footage. Pervasive monitoring of celebrities and political figures has dominated the scoops and scandals of the British tabloid press, as surveillance equipment and paparazzi have come to constitute the source of political information and popular entertainment.[179] The individual is emptied of all agency except their capacity to also become part of consumer entertainment, and so the infantilised masses contemplate themselves as passive spectacle, the signal point of fascism as Walter Benjamin warned.[180] As 'reality' becomes a fixture of television programming, observe a new phenomenon of online self-commodification through Web 2.0 profiling, blogging and use of twitter to immediately share thoughts (and thereby assume their worth), and the rise of home-made pornography. Galloway and Thacker describe this self-commodification with a new motto for the digitised era: 'Express yourself! Output some data!'[181] I in turn LOL and dutifully retweet this, 'Like' its Facebook page, or repost it on my utterly tedious micro-blog.

Recall the discussion of finance earlier as something groundless, no longer earthed to a fixed and tangible standard like gold, as in the case of the US dollar. When language and place are emptied of truth-standards, and are deregulated from the protection of intelligent witnesses and social protections, they too fall into the trap of becoming whirligig projections upon which anyone with the most powerful resources can project disinformation without audits or opposition. The manipulation of information becomes a major architecture of control, a true perversion of language, as a forged consent is generated through political representation. Neoliberalism has been marked by the rise of a specific kind of career-politician, a new kind of self-interested 'Political Class' as Peter Oborne argues. PR expenditure and policy advisers increasingly replace the civil service, judiciary and Parliament in real decision-making.[182] It leads to a cultural slurry of smooth corruption and narrowing ownership and accountability, a 'manipulative populism' as Oborne calls it, as politicians cynically use a language of fairness, choice and security whilst communicating their ideology (and often decisions) via their partners in the mainstream media.[183]

For Oborne, the rising political class signal two dangers: the decline of democratic civil government, as seen in the marginalisation of parliament, the Cabinet and judiciary; and an increasing social and political homogeneity amongst all the political parties which are increasingly converging around the same politics. A term like Nick Clegg's 'radical centre' might hint at this redundancy of political opposition, and Oborne accounts for this homogeneity by politicians cynically targeting only swing voters and by attempting to outmanoeuvre voters/consumers through 'triangulation', an electoral strategy of adopting the opposition's political ideas and exploiting them to make the opponent look extremist on them – a practice of imitation that accounts for the policy convergence of Labour, Liberal Democrats and Conservatives since 1997, if not earlier.[184] Meaningful consent is cemented amongst an elite media and business leaders through regular private meetings at the Prime Minister's home.[185] Faced with funding shortages and declining memberships, political parties now rely on corporate funding and donations which are rewarded by access to ministers and frequently honours.[186] Cynically, politicians have defended their own hegemony using a language of justice, modernity, meritocracy and fairness, to which this quote from Tony Blair in 2001 is indicatively empty of meaning:

Arrayed against us: the forces of conservatism, the cynics, the elites, the establishment. Those who will live with decline. Those who yearn for yesteryear. Those who just can't be bothered. Those who prefer to criticise rather than do. On our side, the forces of modernity and justice.[187]

Blair is the embodiment of the fundamental hypocrisy and insincerity of contemporary politicians. The Political Class pitches itself as radical against the establishment, offering a new kind of freedom all the while its networks and mechanisms of control pervade through national government. An obvious neoliberal consensus of opinion has been established in Westminster, whose discord is frequently exaggerated in the popular press. Manipulative populism reflects what Castells describes as the permeation of media into politics, where 'Leadership is personalized, and image-making is power-making'.[188] Voters are unable to make a meaningful political choice, and so vote increasingly on the perceived personality of the party leader, or more often based on the defects of the opposition party – as most recently demonstrated in the 2010 election, to the detriment of the seemingly-morose and aloof Gordon Brown against the utterly superficial 'new politics' of Clegg and Cameron. In either case, government by neoliberal ideas was ensured. This forged consent, attack on the judiciary and the civil service, as well as the decline of an independent political press brings the UK in the early 21st century tremulously closer to a vulnerability to fascism.

Nick Davies further underlines a forged consent between media, politicians and the electorate in his vast internal research into the production of news. He also offers a pessimistic vision of a news industry dominated by a shrinking number of increasingly powerful media magnates, who are increasingly eroding the truth-telling capacity of journalism for production values motivated only by profit, leading to mass-output of unresearched, unqualified, unoriginal and highly rushed reportage, or 'churnalism'.[189] Davies provides compelling evidence of how even the major British broadsheet newspapers rely on PR statements and one major internal news-wire for the majority of their news reports, the Press Association, as well as relying on the international news-wires of the Associated Press and Reuters. Davies and Cardiff University researchers found that during a two-week period only 12% of domestic stories in the top five reputable UK newspapers could be demonstrated as written by reporters themselves. Shockingly, 60% were wholly reproductions of news-wire or PR statements; 20% involved some major trace of these, and 8% were indeterminable.[190] This leads to a monopolisation of information, sold and transmitted from a shrinking pool of companies (News International, Press Association, or from digitised information management companies like Apple, Google, Getty Images, Amazon, Microsoft), which generates an increasingly distorted and singular view of political events. Information is the most essential commodity of abstractive, negative capitalism. Information has become enclosed by a shrinking number of media magnates, demonstrated using an Internet example in the vertical shift of information from Usenet groups of distributed nodes to increasingly centralised 'cloud computing' where information is hosted by a small amount of companies with the capacity to manage and store this data for free. As information becomes homogenised, individual data becomes vulnerable to hacking and deletion – the potential disappearance of one's digital identity altogether.

The danger of such a homogenisation is entropy: a system becomes vulnerable to corruption by contaminating viruses. A monopolised information network is gullible to cunning hackers and disinformation piracy, such as the Yes Men's 2004 announcement (impersonating Dow Chemical) that it would liquidate Union Carbide, the company responsible for the deadly 1984 Bhopal Disaster, using the $12 billion this would generate towards medical care for those 120 000 affected.[191] The company quickly lost $2 billion in share values as investors panicked at the prospect of a capitalist company using their wealth for an altruistic end. The system of PR can therefore be manipulated with counter-PR, as the Yes Men and others demonstrate, contaminating market confidence rapidly, spreading quickly and immediately throughout the network, a powerful corruption of language that even Deleuze was optimistic enough to foresee as a weapon against control societies.[192]

The language of the Political Class is increasingly vacated of semantic meaning, be it in the near schizoid-repetition of 'pure and simple' or 'fairness' by Cameron; or 'new' or 'modernising' by Blair.[193] Meaningless is incorrect: it speaks authority, control and the interests of political party donors, as language itself becomes also 'expropriated' and 'alienated' by capitalism, as Agamben puts it.[194] This language presents no information except the authority of the government, leading to a kind of Orwellian 'doublespeak', such as in Cameron's recent cynical attack on welfare and poverty itself as producing a culture of poverty, for which the neoliberal response is to remove (expensive) welfare support and other social support packages in order to seemingly end poverty.[195] Such a move is palpably ridiculous, but such statements made often enough, authoritatively enough and through repetition become mantra. This system effects ultimate control by removing social support structures whilst convincing voters this is for their own benefit, indeed empowering them with more freedom in a 'big society'. In neoliberal parlance, a 'free' service is a privatised and marketised one, free to no-one except she (though most often he) who owns property rights on it. As Cameron put it:

> So let me tell you what our change looks like. It's about ending the old big government, top-down way of running public services ... releasing the grip of state control and

putting power in people's hands. The old dogma that said Whitehall knows best – it's gone. There will be more freedom, more choice and more local control. Ours is a vision of open public services.[196]

Neoliberalism exchanges open public services for closed services; involves the increasing handover of public money into private hands despite the devastating legacy of New Labour's abortive PFI schemes as well as the recent collapse of home-care providers Southern Cross, and ultimately enacts a far more controlling political intervention into the running of local services than previous governments might have attempted.[197] As a declaration of control, it shares neoliberal theory's active state intervention in 'freeing' markets, as well as a cynical offer of choice and advantages where such decisions can only result in further redundancies and irreversible cutbacks to local services, now tightened by a profit-seeking agenda. Another example comes in the recent Home Office's 'New Approach to Fighting Crime' of March 2011. Here a language of crime-fighting superheroes is used alongside declarations that government itself has interfered too much in regulating these services. The report fundamentally transforms the police service's priorities, despite noisily rejecting any intervention from big government: the purpose of policing shifts from solving crime to now fighting and 'cutting' crime, as well as 'tackling anti-social behaviour'.[198] As the report puts it, the 'police do an excellent job but the rise in bureaucracy, targets and paperwork under the last Government turned the police into form-writers instead of crime-fighters'.[199] The previous New Labour government are rebuked in red-top tabloid terms, whilst the causes of criminal behaviour are attributed to individual defects instead of social problems.

This report supplies the final points for my account of manipulative populism as a strategy of negative capitalism. As an economic politic, neoliberalism flexes its hegemony through a cynical language of security or terrorist threats to establish further control mechanisms. It employs arguments of individual irresponsibility to punish and blame the poor, whilst attacking 'big government' itself in a veiled shift to removing the state's social functions, turning the modern Western state into a tax-regulating organisation for the protection of the wealthy, increasing expenditure only in order to increase security internally, wage war externally, and develop social areas in order to re-channel further private investment, such as the London 2012 Olympics. Neoliberalism becomes a peculiarly nationalistic ideology in order to manage the libidinal discontent of its increasingly-impoverished and anxious populations. Who could object to choice, or freedom, or empowering local communities? Further neoliberal reforms are pushed through manipulated consent like a Trojan horse, a harmless gift offering for which UK citizens will pay heavily for in debt over coming years, as further privatisation and decreasing individual rights are pushed through via a semantically meaningless and deceptive language of freedom, choice and security.

The danger of data abstraction, an inevitable consequence of coding all life into financial capital and digitised information, is one's vulnerability to identity theft or identity loss. Heather Brooke calls this a 'data doppelgänger' – the terrifying Kafkaesque scenario where due to administrative errors, one's name is incorrectly input on a database from which one's real name and identity cannot be recovered.[200] This is finally seen through a negation of democratic agency into a cynical forged consent. In the control society, information is a commodity and ignorance the mark of proletarianisation. This is eerily best articulated by Edward Bernays, the American creator of Public Relations as a field, and the leading developer of psychoanalytic techniques in marketing and political campaigning, back in 1928:

In almost every act of our daily lives, whether in the sphere of politics of business, in our social conduct or our ethical thinking, we are dominated by the relatively small number of persons ... who pull the wires which control the public mind.[201]

In this 'invisible government' of PR fabrications one falls into the position of Joseph K., condemned outright to ignorance. There is a particular scene worth repeating where the Village superintendent tells K. that the Castle can never be mistaken on any matter, only that its pronouncements should not always be taken literally, the ultimate perversion of language:

'So the only remaining conclusion,' said K., 'is that everything is very uncertain and insoluble, including my being thrown out.' 'Who would take the risk of throwing you out, Land Surveyor?' asked the Superintendent. 'The very uncertainty about your summons guarantees you the most courteous treatment, only you're too sensitive by all appearances. Nobody keeps you here, but that surely doesn't amount to throwing you out.[202]

Negative capitalism denies even the possibility of sure information about one's status, as one's data-identity, visa, job or community can become deleted at any time. Uncertainty has become the collective experience of British citizens in the early 21st century, a citizenship defined by debt, anxiety, depression and the psychological need for security, consumer consolations and seemingly-strong government. Political language has been perverted into non-meaning as political parties become increasingly homogeneous and defensive of their wealthy funders. Representative democracy in the UK is now a manufactured fiction, a grubby façade that conceals the more effective invisible government of financial capital.

Rather than retreat into angst-ridden alienation, British

workers can sidestep existing structures. Political deception and manipulation can be overcome like all forms of corrupt and bad management by establishing a new secular constitution and civil law, by all and for all, where the democratic body is heard and speaks without tyrannical dominion. Alternative democratic arrangements should be made, new and independent 'parliaments' could be initiated, formed by democratic communities based on locality. With the power of information technologies, the need for representative MPs to sit in discussions of fat jeering men is now irrelevant: referenda can be conducted on a regular basis like online or TV polls. Votes might be made not by individuals pressing buttons at home, but by the collective agreement of democratic communities who meet and vote on decisions. By participating in a constitution, one becomes a citizen and is imbued with the responsibilities and rights of public citizenship. Although like the words of Cameron all this is merely speculative hot air, without affirming an alternative the modern subject returns to the precarious uncertainty analysed in this chapter, an uncertainty that leads to the new cynicism of Generation Meh.

7

Generation Meh

Already, meh. The sheer effort of writing about modern cynicism, or reading about it, could possibly kill me. I just cannot be bothered. Everything is so tiring, so tired, and so pointless. What's happening on Facebook? In the news? – no, reading takes too long, there's just too much information. Meh to all that.

Georg Wilhelm Friedrich Hegel offers a total description of truth, that historical progress is always made in dialectical struggle whereby the Abstract or truth (thesis) must encounter its Negative or error (antithesis), which is finally overcome to reach the Concrete (synthesis, *aufheben*).[203] No new mode of power sweeps through without some kind of psychological or libidinal opposition. In the contemporary era, the grinding negation of work and consumption naturally meets a powerful resistance of humour, integrity, and solidarity. A resolution or synthesis is achieved in cynicism, the neoliberal condition, which allows discontent and desire for alternative ways of living to be expressed harmlessly on a daily basis through bad jokes, anti-intellectualism, and meh. Cynicism is the perverted psychological resistance of the modern individual, one that refuses to believe in governments or media, but refuses to do anything about misrule and misinformation either. Cynicism is a powerful armour that binds the individual together in affected indifference against excessive flows of images, advertisements and information. But who wins in this process? Is it capital which is abstract truth and the individual which is the negative? Or the abstracted individual who is truth, life, and who now comes up against the negative of capitalism? Either way, cynicism offers an insight into how an effective opposition to negative capitalism can be understood in practice, though to speak of only one kind of cynicism seems incorrect given the many different ways it is commonly understood, from ignorant indifference or disaffected disappointment to an informed callousness. Here cynicism is broken down into new categories: *resentment, collective fatalism,* and *dividualism.*

How does one begin to present such a collective judgement of the psychological mindset of negative capitalism? Cynicism firstly offers both a description of a unique deferral of judgement and agency whilst being complicit to facts: like in Franz Kafka's *The Castle,* a Castle official who may not agree or understand why the Land Surveyor cannot be assigned a status, but accepts that this alone is the case, that the reasons why the decision have been made cannot and should not be understood, that to attempt to understand them would end in failure anyway, and that ultimately one must accede to facts, if not truths – bureaucratic nihilism.[204] Fisher offers a more specific bureaucratic example of the Further Education college manager who instructs him to lie about his own self-assessment exercise, writing a vacuous self-critique of his performance, not because the procedure has any reflective value, but because it needed to look like it had been completed properly, that is, with a certain 'virtuosity', using Virno's expression from earlier.[205] There are countless cases of bureaucratic absurdities that obey the letter of the law rather than the spirit, but Virno can help to elaborate what exactly unites these states. He describes how the 'bad sentiments' of opportunism and cynicism pervade the multitude, who experience rules instead of facts or events.[206] Cultural life, labour practices or political structures seem groundless, modulated only by rules one must follow – no-one has specifically elected this system of practices, and no-one has any sense of how they might be altered, or if they even should – but they are experienced as a kind of game. Where nothing is either true or false, where no stable position is ever possible, or even desirable, what does one strive for? There is only brutal and cynical self-affirmation, a naked virtuosity of success in what is a rigged competition.

"Money makes the world go round" becomes the rule, a statement uttered with a sigh, and the cynical response is to accept that only passive consent and self-affirmation can afford one any measure of success in this world, however unstable it may actually be. Thus cruel and crushed cynicism is the mark of resentment of those who have abandoned the possibility of change. This abandonment of the burdens of history and of truth, a self-abandonment, is intoxicating in the way one drowns one's sorrows. Cynicism liberates the modern individual from the burdens of taking responsibility for transforming society, a mass 'consensual hallucination' of melancholia, as Pasquinelli calls it.[207] This refuge in resentment has been detected at numerous fault-lines: Pascal Bruckner finds a masochistic narcissism in the West's guilt over its colonial heritage, echoing the misanthropic white male European angst of Michel Houellebecq's novels ("it's all our fault").[208] But though money may make the world go round, this is an unwanted series of relations whose rule, but not validity, is resentfully accepted. It is a disavowal that permeates the system, but a disavowal which has yet to become open disobedience. Benjamin Noys and Fredric Jameson have both suggested that within the *ressentiment* of the proletariat lies a palpable and violent negativity which might undo neoliberal capitalism.[209] When democratic bodies of angry workers start rioting and creating new and autonomous social democratic organisations, the security guards, CCTV-operatives, underpaid soldiers and temp scab workers might not be arsed to stand in their way.

Peter Sloterdijk's 1983 *Critique of Cynical Reason* provides a more sympathetic and insightful introduction into this modern condition of cynicism. He describes it as a kind of borderline melancholia that allows its sufferer to continue working whilst passively acceding and distancing themselves from the validity of ethics and social judgements.[210] From the semantic meaning-lessness of the conscientious statesman's public utterance, to the bawdy satirical laughter heard in community pubs and clubs, modern cynicism shields itself from the 'naivety' of universal laws to a depressive self-protection within the ironic treatment of language.[211] The modern cynic cannot really believe in the value of what they do, or that they have any meaningful political agency, but this naked fact cannot be openly confessed either. In a cynical era, utopia is replaced by ruin and catastrophe; cheerful and cheeky truth-seeking affirmation is replaced with a cold, hard-lipped demoralisation and retreat into narcissism. Within the history of ideas, a cynical era is one where 19th century positivism, with its faith in universal enlightenment, has been replaced with a late 20th century nihilism, with a collapse of moral sense into indeterminate deconstruction and truth as a functional value alone.[212] Sloterdijk's account is intentionally provocative of its immediately middle-class 'post-socialist' European audience, but provides a good description of collective fatalism. Decision-making is deferred and postponed by the precarity and insecurity of modern living, something discussed in Chapter Six, but wider political decisions about market regulation, political organisation or cultural change are also deferred and postponed by the immediate demands of production.

Sloterdijk describes this postponement as a uniquely Western phenomenon, reminding us momentarily of Max Weber and the Protestant work ethic, which Sloterdijk silently acknowledges here: 'Before we "really live," we always have just one more matter to attend to, just one more precondition to fulfill, just one more temporarily more important wish to satisfy, just one more account to settle'.[213] Collective fatalism is a mass belief that meaningful change is impossible, with individuals deferring decision-making in the expectation someone else will make them on their behalf, with or without their consent. This leads to an infantilisation as citizens enjoy their disempowerment as consumers alone, a new 'major psychological shift' as Ballard calls it, whereby shopping replaces voting as the final, meaningful act of affirmation, signalling a new boredom that, lacking alternatives, leads to fascism.[214]

This cynicism also rationally justifies what is an unbearable circumstance: that the Enlightenment notions of transparent democratic government, civil liberty, public commons, meaningful consent and social happiness have been forcibly negated by the increasing anxiety, debt, depression and control architectures of neoliberal capitalism. Rather than initiate a psychologically traumatic and seemingly unwinnable struggle against these circumstances, this melancholia is rationalised with a collective fatalism and a sigh: "oh well, we sort of tried, now pass me over the Ben and Jerry's and the Sky Plus remote". Kafka was unable to complete his struggle against *The Castle*, though it is thought that had he ever returned to complete the work, Joseph K. would have abandoned his struggle for recognition and would instead have died peacefully in the Village, a note from the Castle announcing on his deathbed that his claim to live in the village was not legally valid, but given auxiliary circumstances he would be permitted to live and work there.[215] Like *The Trial*, this is a psychological work about the modern self never getting what it wants: recognition; sexual liaison as Deleuze and Guattari suggest; or marriage as his letter to his father spells out – happiness, fundamentally.[216] Perhaps the ultimate optimistic resistance to such a cynical collective fatalism was never to finish the work.

Every self-consciously 'modern' era has been racked by angst concerning dangerously increasing selfishness, narcissism and greed, and I am wary of exhorting a modern Savonarola-style bonfire of the iPhones. But the third current of contemporary cynicism is 'dividualism', using Deleuze's term earlier: the purchases and productivity of the individual are celebrated and affirmed but without any grounding to an existential self. Dividualism is a cynical distancing away from the social concerns and communitarian beliefs of the Fordist post-war consensus and its socialised politic, for an internalisation of the self-seeking consumerist and money-motivated ideals of the economic politic of neoliberalism. Its incessant credit-fuelled consumption is marked by what Fisher calls a 'depressive anhedonia', a compulsive pleasure-seeking that is incapable of satisfaction, an impulse to always spend, become intoxicated, check emails and social network websites incessantly in order to fend off the insatiable bother of boredom.[217] Its atomisation is marked by the growth of home-based entertainment technologies, the increasing practice of drinking alcohol and watching sporting or entertainment events at home. Its politics are defined by an increasing anxiety over security, be it a fear of street crime or parasitic immigration, both moral panics keenly fostered by the popular British press over the last thirty years and shaping the outcomes of general election results.[218]

Dividualism concurs with John Prescott's announcement that 'we are all middle class now': during an era of rapidly increasing social inequality where a FTSE 100 CEO is paid 145 times the average wage, the 2011 High Pay Commission found that the majority of British adults surveyed tended to overestimate their own wealth and underestimate or entirely misunderstand the earnings of the top 0.1% of the wealthy.[219] It attributed this increasing wealth divide as due to a mixture of declining trade union power, increasing individualism throughout society, and unspecified 'social and cultural changes'.[220] The 2011 British Social Attitudes Survey has also found an increasing sympathy for those on low-incomes, but with that a declining support for wealth redistribution by the government, and an increasing hostility to those dependent on welfare.[221] It is a cynicism formed out of the crudest pessimism. On the one hand, the High Pay Commission noted growing distrust of business: since 1998 those with no confidence in business had increased by 7% to 26% of those surveyed; whilst a 2009 EU report found that 74% of UK citizens surveyed believed that corruption was 'widespread' in British politics, following the revelations of the MPs Expenses scandal of that year, a corruption and cynicism further compounded by the revelations of collusion and bribery between journalists, politicians and the Metropolitan police during the '#hackgate' scandal since in 2011.[222] Despite this damning lack of confidence in the ruling classes, a pessimistic dividualism has so far hamstrung disaffection from festering into any meaningful lasting revolt yet. It is a cynicism which attributes sole culpability and possibility in the individual, one that has lost all optimism in collective social or political transformation.

Dividualism is the psychological internalisation of the economic ideals of negative capitalism, it relishes and enjoys its technologies, the apparent freedom offered. It is also 'kynical' however in the way Sloterdijk suggests – it mocks taking politics or anything seriously, disdains social explanations for individual ones, abandoning social ideals when bargains are offered.[223] An analogy to video games, its increasing leisure pursuit, is apt: dividualism plays social reality like World of Warcraft or The Sims, where life is a game to be played, that involves cynically completing banal tasks in order to buy new clothes or items, expand one's property gradually, and to perform life in a safe, controllable setting away from the disintegrating social relationships and political economies that surround workers. It is the justification of selfish and aggressive competition, implied in the urban middle-class 'Chelsea Tractor' that destroys cyclists and the atmosphere in order for insecure wealthy city-dwellers to dominate the roads in expensive Jeeps; it is also implied in the increasing popularity over the last ten years in working-class communities to keep violent fighting dogs like the Staffordshire Bull Terrier. Dividualism is the death reprise of Western citizens who have not realised that cheap credit may be over, that ecological collapse is likely, and its politics is now driving the resentful politics of xenophobic political parties achieving increasing electoral success across Europe and the US since 2008. Dividualism is finally glimpsed in the inadequate resistance strategies of Southwood, who calls for 'camp humour' to beat neoliberal labour practices; or Noys who demands a notion of 'courage' borrowed from Western movies for those who wish to wreak negativity against neoliberal capital.[224] Like the prescriptions of psychopharmacology and CBT, all expect positive change to occur from the rational mindset of the individual. Instead, in perhaps the ultimate cynical twist, life must not be considered as altruistic or fundamentally good. It is ultimately a test of how serious one is about collectively realising one's own truth and desire before financial capitalism sets the agenda for each of us. Do each of us want the burden of responsibility for the world around us? Perhaps not. But if so, then serious collective and democratic strategies are required to resist the motion of cynical dividualism towards consumerist, atomised fascism. Social democracy will not be a peaceful birth, but a devious and innovative awakening.

8

New Flesh: Non-places and Gonzo Porn

Place and time disappear under the burden of their own contradictions: the worker must be switched on and available to labour at all hours. If one is not driving away at one of a number of small projects, one is expected to be networking or upgrading one's skill-set. The modern home, workplace and sites of pleasure have become 'non-places', colonised by work, where one is no longer 'at home', alienated in that sense described by Virno earlier. Life itself becomes crammed into bedsits, laptops, productive behaviours, and glimpses of furtive sleep stolen during nocturnal hours.[225] Marc Augé coined the term 'non-place' back in 1990 to describe the loss of place in a society at the service of financial capital, a feeling of loss that paralleled the wider defeat of political socialism and a decline of community spaces and civic spirit. The only things created in non-place communities are billboards, betting shops, chain supermarkets, and surveillance posts. This is the utopia of negative capitalism (where *utopia* technically rendered from Greek to English means a *not-place*), where everything apparently is available and possible to each of us, and beneath the possible are debts, retail assistant work, and endemic depression. Places lacking identity, interaction, based only on private consumption fit into ideas of utopia and offer in turn psychological rewards of safety, hygiene and control. What else is there to do in the out-of-town retail park community except watch TV, take part in the resentful politics of friends, and look round the shops? This then informs what counts as 'relaxation' when not working.

For Augé, urban late modernity or 'supermodernity' is defined by a loss of 'place', a location with which one has an 'anthropological' and relational identity.[226] Why did place and its loss cause such anxiety? For Augé, 'non-places are the real measure of our time', areas of the city defined by a lack of human interaction and solitary anonymity: the airport, the motorway, the hotel, the underground car-park, the shopping centre, the vast network of signs that direct, instruct and regulate the flows of these places, as well as communication networks.[227] These interzones designate and dissociate humans into functions of 'solitary contractuality', so that points of public interaction, play, rest, are bled away as unnecessary, dangerous or criminal. In the non-places of modernity one's proper functions are revealed: to work and to consume, stripped of the burdens of identity. As Augé puts it, the citizen of the non-place 'becomes no more than what he does or experiences in the role of passenger, customer or driver...He tastes for a while...the passive joys of identity-loss, and the more active pleasure of role-playing'.[228]

Calling these now-mundane social sites 'non-places' is not just a curmudgeonly disregard for modern times. There is pleasure offered too in the mall and in the norm of self-modification, be it through CBT, plastic surgery, or tattooing: in each there is an opportunity to escape through oneself alone. What better consolation for feeling negated? J.G. Ballard is interesting for his relatively early accounts of the exciting libidinal possibilities of identity-loss in the non-place. He is aroused by the new opportunities these distinctly modern sites offer, particularly in his short stories and novels from the 1970s, where the motorway system, motor car, multi-storey car-park, plastic surgery, the airport motel, high-rise luxury flats, or the Mediterranean package holiday become charged with exciting and lethal erotic possibility. The non-place becomes the setting for a strange and disquieting crime or trauma, which is then used to reveal deep-seated desires for violence, cruelty, sex and death beneath bourgeois middle class life.

A new kind of subjectivity emerges out of the architecture of the underground car-park, the motor-car, and the gated community: one that is impulsive, opportunistic, isolated, paranoid, depressed when its desires are unrealised, one that is fundamentally infantilised. Yet unlike Ballard's motorways or underground car-parks, the paradigmatic site of exchange of contemporary modernity is no longer 'present', unless in a digitised and immaterial sense. Those places which are not-places, and which define the constricted communities and commons of social, political and cultural exchange are now online – the invisible and distant financial exchanges for instance, facilitated by machinic algorithms, derivatives and other electronic financial products. Online sexualities are far more prominent and charged compared to the spectral isolation and violent sexualities of the motor car and the car-park. There is a new erotic potential, banality and grubbiness in online sex-chat, DIY porn, live web-cam sex encounters and new online personas. In each case, identity loss is the goal – to escape one's drearily ordinary appearance, to get out of one's head – which explains why the average British town-centre, the site of the public, is defined by shopping by day, and drinking by night, each to excess. The task that Ballard undertook, and which Augé introduced, is why this has become the general intellect of the neoliberal era. If a mass democratic revolt can be initiated, the causes of identity-loss will need to be disrupted. There will be no class consciousness or social democratic revolt if each man or woman is still dreaming about dancing, singing or joking on stage to a Saturday night TV drudge nation.

Let's ask instead: what desires were met or agreements made that brought about this socio-cultural shift from an organised, often self-educated working-class citizen to a disorganised marketplace of consumer-democracy? How did qualifications replace qualities? That is not to suggest that some forgotten referendum occurred in the early 1980s when such a decision was collectively and consciously made in the UK, perhaps after a bleary Campari-stained Eurovision song contest. But it is undeniable to someone born during or before the Thatcher years that a marked shift in the working-class usage of public spaces occurred from the 1980s onwards. A visit to the new Westfield East mall reveals some of the benefits of these non-places: organised, clearly-demarcated, hygienically clean and protected from the elements, secure from intruders, offering a comfortable and egalitarian alienation from the nuisance of other human beings. A display is knocked over: someone will clear it up without asking, without a pleasantry or apology. Equal customer service is offered to all consumers, regardless of rudeness or the question concerned. Benches are offered for seating too, rather than the playschool-oversized and uncomfortable chairs that now feature in public squares. The mall space offers an illusion of openness whilst being under heavy surveillance.

Opinions on politics or current affairs in the mall are disdained in favour of the coarse moral prejudices that inform most political opinion, an effect of an increasingly-uniform Political class, alongside the frames of 'sleaze', 'justice' and 'rights' which have shaped popular political discourse in the UK over the last thirty years. The popularity of the mall reflects the importance of the *X-Factor* TV talent show for understanding why such entertainment shows attract more votes and viewers than general elections, despite the fairly equal evidence of fraud and cynicism behind the management of both. The validity of the consumer (shopper or viewer's) opinion is not questioned – everyone has an equal vote on contestants, provided they follow the show and phone in. Mockery of the more gullible candidates who humiliate themselves on the show whets the viewer's interest; in between the hero and the fool, a superficially heart-warming rags-to-riches tale of a singing grandma. The alienation induced by the mall or personal technologies allows the viewer to equally enjoy all social relations only insofar as they affect us alone. Life itself becomes a jittery on-demand TV show one can solicit up. Actions lack consequences.

In J.G. Ballard's final novel *Kingdom Come*, cable TV and the Metro-Centre shopping mall are ultimately the main actors in the novel, without which so little could happen. Curious this, given that TV and the mall are indeed too disciplinary sites, limited by timetables and store opening hours, compared to the continuous possibilities of online shopping and downloaded TV to phones and computers, increasingly becoming the normal manner of consumption. But the centrality and importance of these technologies remains unabated, and instead demand is increased for continual availability. Faced with the TV-image of a future one is unable to switch off or switch-over from, Ballard asks us to 'Think of the future as a cable TV programme going on for ever'.[229] Life is repeatedly compared to a TV commercial, whilst with Wildean rancour Ballard later snipes that 'They've been educated by TV commercials. They know that the only things with any value are those that can be put in a carrier bag. This is a plague area'.[230] Antonin Artaud described the onset of plague in Europe as a 'psychic entity', embodying a real crisis of culture which could only be resolved by death or cure.[231] Artaud's rabid observation was not intended as metaphor, but as analogy plague offers an excellent way of conceiving the nascent crisis in contemporary culture, when ruins and riots can only be contemplated with either cynical disgust or arousal, and where the possibility of the future as progressive ideal has been forgotten or abandoned. Poverty drives one to value only that which one brutally lacks: money, basic commodities, healthy and varied foods, an education, time to think and reflect. No future life or alternative is offered – there are TV commercials, TV talent shows, and little else.

In the *X-Factor* and the mall, everyone gets to text or email in with their opinion, 'Like' or jeer what they glimpse amidst the intense media-effluence of homogeneous styles and tastes, so long as they never question their validity. The real decisions are made elsewhere. Nothing except my own inability to obtain further credit and overdrafts will restrict me from these pleasures. The mall and the *X-Factor* protect the modern ego against the traumas of negative capitalism whilst subtly reinforcing them through their frame of consumerism as social relation – in an economic politic I am no longer a citizen but a customer and a client. I take time off from working to buy fashionable clothing on credit, or drink a standard coffee from a standard coffee-shop. In the neoliberal economic model, spending is working, and by reinvesting my wage into the consumer economy I am investing in the leisure-based future of myself and my peers. I aspire to make myself feel better by buying new clothes, boozing regularly, ordering DVD box sets and books I have no time to look at, taking antidepressants, and scrimping aside enough money for a holiday and a reserve for the next period of unemployment. The frequency of mirrors increases at a time of mass individuality, when everyone spends money to look the same. The flesh is a site of erotic escapism, only provided someone else is watching and validating the act with their gaze.

Pornography offers insight into this relation in three ways. Firstly, users themselves are increasingly becoming the subject of DIY pornography, discernible in the increasing popularity of gonzo porn and free Porn 2.0 websites like LiveJasmin, YouPorn, xHamster, Pornhub and so on.[232] The former expertise of the adult movie star, informed expert or hard-working singer-songwriter is abandoned for a free contest of amateurs. The increasing necessity of the close-up on the act of fucking is indicative, particularly in gonzo porn – the focus and process the viewer is being aroused by is no longer the expected money-shot but the piston-motions of fisting and penetration, inducing an especially gynaecological perspective to achieve sexual climax. The body is no longer a sublime object but abstracted flesh, consisting of a stable economy of drives that must be relieved. An efficient sexuality assessed by quantities, of orgasms, of sessions of intercourse. Saturation in affects and an increasing disinhibition between strangers, provided screens act as intermediaries, leads to smartphone apps like Grindr where free consensual sex (among gay men) can be procured during a lunchbreak. Finally, the money shot now seems archaic, a quotation of more quaint 1980s tastes, a sign of "job done" for the phallocentric gaze. To achieve orgasm the pornographic lens now needs the ecstatic eye of the amateur actor or actress gazing back into the camera lens and signalling full pleasure in the act, marking the shift here to affective labour – how can the viewer be sure that this is an authentic orgasm, and not one faked?[233] Vestiges of animality or sense are removed: the performers are shaven, fashionably underdressed, and are fucked with viagra callousness by old men. The viewer must see the genitals and fluids in anatomical detail to be assured of credibility. Getting one over is the aim in gonzo porn, where narrative arcs generally focus on duping young girls into sex acts they would not otherwise consent to. Whether it is actually an authentic or faked orgasm is irrelevant, so long as it appears so and consents with increasingly distorted expectations of what the sexual body can provide.

Individual sexuality is explained and determined by the social and economic conditions of class conflicts. As much as I might think my pornographic preferences are my own, they are formed out of the availability and fashions of production, hence changes in capitalist production lead to a change in pornographic tastes. The fundamental social error of negative capitalism is permitting economy to produce society, rather than permitting society to produce and manage the economy. At present economy produces society and its terms of being, where capital/power entirely pervades life and alienates it into purely economic and productive behaviours. Against Laurie Penny's recent *Meat Market*, it is naïve to pose sex or squatted social centres as offering some sacred pre-Fall refuge against capitalist negation:

these speeds and methods already permeate imaginations and practices.[234] The alienation of the sexual and romantic body into an abstracted economy of drives marks a contemporary sexual alienation of negative capitalism. The animalistic and often unwittingly-catholic descriptions of 'the flesh', its scents, howls and meat by young writers like Penny marks the futile attempt to solve this loss of an ideal of intimacy by retreating into some fictional pre-capitalist world. If a pre-Fall world exists, those of us whose minds and social expectations are topographies of capitalism cannot go back to a before we never knew, but a forward beyond, propelled by anger and deviant negativity.

Pornography is more straightforward: instead of a lost or alienated ideal, sex is no longer socialised or sentimentalised to the extent it once was. 'Decadence demands a certain degree of innocence', as Maxted explains to Richard Pearson in *Kingdom Come*.[235] Rather than speaking of this pornography as a loss or a problem, it in fact presents new pleasures and possibilities debarred to previous generations, and is symptomatic of a new cultural shift requiring further analysis. This is the site of the new flesh, where the identity-loss of the non-place is matched by the possibilities of self-modified skin.[236] One of the liberating effects of neoliberal capital is a detaching of identity from fixed and inescapable notions of self. In Francis Bacon's portraits of trapped bodies, Deleuze glimpsed a new '*zone of indiscernibility*' between man and animal, between meat and flesh.[237] The old existential definitions come undone, out of which new possibilities emerge. If revolt can be conceived in a democratic body hooked to the excitement of identity-loss, which it can, provided it engages young people on their terms – then flesh will become indiscernible, intelligent, and entirely responsible for activating a consensual desire. To fuck instead of being fucked, going beyond the passivity of porn workers and hunger-artists that financial capital has made of each of us.

Existential time is a political issue. Alongside a defence of working rights and the value of the public commons, asserting the right to inertia in the non-place, of lazing about, offers political potential, using an unlikely source, Dostoevsky's *Notes from Underground*. 'Last of all, gentlemen: it is best to do nothing! The best thing is conscious inertia! So long live the underground'.[238] Dostoevsky's plea of an impoverished underground man (remember, this is addressed to gentlemen alone) carves open, strangely, a new kind of place within a non-place. This impoverished squalid individual isn't supposed to speak – in fact the novel struggles with the danger of open conflict within a claustrophobic urban environment throughout – but *Notes from Underground* opens up the first existential and angry space of the unspoken, of the unspeakable. A willed and 'conscious inertia', of slowing-down to read, to think, to learn, to eat, to spend time with our friends and loved ones, could cause problems for line managers. If wealth is considered as something based on free time possessed, rather than money (or available credit), a time free of work or worrying about it, then even the more relatively economically-secure might find reason to get angry. Dead time is negativity, therefore negative capitalism is overcome through a politicisation of time and a positive mass campaign towards non-productivity and idleness.

There is already a political reclamation of the non-place occurring, one lacking a name or spearhead but containing a cohesive focus on democratic self-representation. Some of the earlier non-places, such as the Brutalist social housing blocks of the UK, have since the 1990s enjoyed a re-embrace and perhaps reclamation as 'places' of culture. Observe this in TV comedies like Benidorm, in recent British cinema, such as, to pick four examples among many, *Beautiful Thing* (1996), *Fishtank* (2009), *Misfits* (2009-present), or more problematically in *Attack the Block* (2011). A new political potential is discovered and represented in these earlier derided non-places, discernible in Owen Hatherley's defence of British socialism in Brutalist social housing, or in

Laura Oldfield Ford's *Savage Messiah* (2011) drawings of riots against yuppiedromes and gentrification that begin in run-down suburban communities and housing estates. There is a nascent cultural resistance in the artists and thinkers re-grouping around Jacques Derrida's term 'hauntology' like Mark Fisher, or in the largely black working-class vernacular music based on pastiche, aggression and self-expression in the British responses and emulations of US Hip-hop to Jungle, Drum and Bass, Garage, 2-Step and more recently Grime and Dubstep. These musical forms are based on a collage of sounds created by software packages like Logic; rhythmic and bass-driven, created in London suburbs like Croydon, Bow, and Tottenham, and spread via the Internet. The future voices of modernity are to be found in the non-places of the suburbs, in the clash between Skinnyman's 'council estate of mind' with Ballard's coming 'suburb of the soul'.[239]

Lacking any stable notion of the future, or any concrete or collective critique of ideology, debasement gets addictive, ironic, passive aggressive. Resistance and revolt is individualised and internalised, as discussed in terms of cynicism earlier, but it also erupts through the medium of the body, in stress, panic attacks, random acts of violence, skin disorders, or violent master-slave narratives to achieve mutual orgasm amongst exhausted part-time lovers.[240] There is simply less time and space to even think through alternatives, whilst normative and determinative decisions are often made as assumptions by the weary data administrators and financial employees who do not have the time or interest to engage in meaningful reflection. There is of course a democratic potential to retake communities and responsibility for activating a better future, but at present it feels denied.

Paul Mason remarks that at 'the centre of all the protest movements is a new sociological type: the graduate with no future'.[241] One might have made the same argument with the anti-globalisation movement over a decade ago, though since then cynicism and melancholic disempowerment have worsened – the protest actions of the Left have largely failed to disrupt the working of financial capitalism, despite having the sympathy and consent of the democracies from which they erupted. The mass-produced graduate comes out of modernity's driving belief in social progress, which has encouraged young people for centuries to place education and lives at the service of ideas. The arts graduate has studied ideas in order to attain a more meaningful life, job and sense of responsibility, but opportunities for creative productivity beyond the extremely competitive or class-restrictive worlds of advertising and finance are rare. The graduate was seduced by the ideals of a long-gone era, and now awakes in a non-place of possibilities. The options open are whether to fundamentally sabotage the sites of restriction – privatised corporate entertainment zones, financial networks, and banking databases – or whether to continue keeping still, saying much and doing little, remaining loyal to the banal and empty opinions and identity politics of Ikea and the mall. Inaction leads to melancholy, and ours is a time of profound melancholia and cynicism, with a dark pleasure in contemplating its own demise in the ruin. It is a decadence that signals that young people no longer feel connected with the future around them, a melancholy that could exhaust itself into creative and vicious anger.

What is this contemporary fixation with ruinporn? The term comes from the case of deindustrialised Detroit, and the increasingly popular phenomena of glossy photographs of its grand and gutted factories like the Packard, the dilapidated Central Michigan station, as well as former-residences given over to lank grasses or even urban farming.[242] Ruinporn describes the exploitative creation and usage of images of poverty and decay. What is exploited is not so much the places themselves but the histories and contexts underlying them, often of multi-racial, or working-class and public settlements, which are whitewashed in favour of glossy, sensationalised and occasionally fabricated images of catastrophe or neglect.[243] Whilst in Detroit there are numerous paradigmatic cases of ruinporn, the arousal that comes from taking and contemplating images of decay and disaster is far more general.[244] Whilst not all abandonment photography is ruinporn – some of it is innocuously historical, the excitement with these exploitative images of ruins and decay comes from a particular ironic disregard for contexts and sociological explanations underlying the image, often leading to their falsification or exaggeration by largely white middle-class photographers who have no interest or connection to the areas they depict. As opposed to photographic collections of abandonment with a historical purpose, ruinporn offers an effective and immediate way for young photographers to get their work noticed and circulating. The practice of photography itself requires a sufficient income and middle-class endorsement that defines the privileged backgrounds of most ruinporn photographers, keen to capture the image of neglect and not the contexts (deindustrialisation, local government spending cuts) behind it. The objects of decay become naked in their abjection. Such images of ruins provide an aesthetic arousal in disaster. Understanding the psychological pleasures behind ruinporn, Susan Sontag's essay on science-fiction offers some parallel insight into the pleasure of catastrophe. Whilst comparing science-fiction films to books and the sensuous elaboration the former offer, Sontag's remarks easily apply to ruin photography:

> In the films it is by means of images and sounds, not words that have to be translated by the imagination, that one can participate in the fantasy of living through one's own death and more, the death of cities, the destruction of humanity itself.[245]

These images are steeped in the aesthetics of destruction, the titillation of havoc, and more significantly, the opportunity for release from everyday obligations to consumer capital. All this will end. The middle-class image-makers of ruinporn gulp in these melancholy slices of "real life" with a certain sexual pleasure, perhaps articulated by a rapturous Keats in "Ode on a Grecian Urn":

> Thou still unravish'd bride of quietness,
> Thou foster-child of silence and slow time.[246]

One advocate of ruinporn sees in these contemporary images of decay a classic 're-enchantment' of the world. Rather drearily echoing the high verse of Keats, Rob Horning has it that

> We want the banal structures and scenes of our everyday life dignified by the patina of decay, so that we can imagine ourselves as noble, mythic Greeks and Romans to a later age and, more important, so that we can better tolerate the frequently shoddy and trite material culture that consumerism foists on us, see it once again as capable of mystery.[247]

The popularity of ruins (and inversely heritage) amongst middle-class viewers reflects an opportunity to confront one's own death as aesthetic spectacle. The pleasure in reflecting on the finitude of existence is an old one, as Keats reminds above, but simply seeing images of deindustrialisation and decay as aesthetic spectacle in the contemporary context betrays the cynicism and (self-)denial of political agency which are specific effects of negative capitalism. With their additional insistence on neglect, these images also absolve the middle-class from any kind of blame or responsibility for these effects of deindustrialisation, suburbanisation (particularly in America), or government cuts caused by tax-breaks for wealthy voters, or changes in aesthetic, architectural or ideological fashions, be they in Detroit, or among the lost 'cosmic' futurism of the Soviet Union recently collected by Frédéric Chaubin, or in the role of gentrification or changing social policy behind the abandonment of Brutalist housing estates of Britain before demolition or gentrification.[248] These images are additionally motivated and produced by largely white middle-class outsiders who see the ruins as pioneers, particularly in the largely Afro-American inner city of Detroit, where racist ideas about murder and crime have inversely made the inner cities attractive to white suburb-bred youth, rebelling against parental warnings.[249] In a discussion of sadism, pornography and the appeals of ruin, there is no better source than the Marquis De Sade's *120 Days of Sodom* for an insight into how wretchedness is necessary for an aristocratic hard-on. In the midst of an orgy, De Sade in typical fashion begins dissertating on matters of happiness and philosophy, with the character of Durcet, a financier, explaining to the Bishop how there is nothing more voluptuous or flattering to the senses than contemplating the tears of those stricken by misery. Durcet explains his inability to reach orgasm in the bountiful excess of the castle thus:

there is one essential thing lacking to our happiness. It is the pleasure of comparison, a pleasure which can only be born of the sight of wretched persons, and here one sees none at all. It is from the sight of him who does not in the least enjoy what I enjoy, and who suffers, that comes the charm of being able to say to oneself: 'I am therefore happier than he'.[250]

Even more darkly comic, Durcet goes on to explain that he has deliberately reduced families to begging in order to enjoy their poverty more. Such fabrications and sexual arousal in the disgust of poverty reminds me of the cynicism of language by contemporary British politicians discussed earlier. De Sade's aristocracy, like the earlier eroticism and exuberance of the aristocrats in Boccaccio's *Decameron* written in the midst of the Black Death, find deepest excessive pleasure by being steeped in the spectacle of their own end. The French aristocracy were in the process of being guillotined; Boccaccio's nobles had somehow survived what felt like the end of the world, annihilating a third of Europeans; so then the middle-class image-makers of these ruins are facing their own proletarianisation and decline in privilege as inflation, frozen wages and continual economic decline leave the middle-classes with the value of their properties and little else. Imagine showing to urban secondary school youth these images of ruined Detroit, or London's abandoned factories or housing estates: I'd bet that there's less likely to be a gee-whiz response or a baited denunciation of gentrification, and more the honest truth of these images, that they depict poverty, deindustrialisation, and little else. For the middle-class makers and consumers of ruinporn there is a deeper cultural arousal in these images: one that objectifies poverty, disregards its real sociological contexts, and comes to relish the fabricated 'authenticity' of misery.

Hatherley's recent journeys around the architecture of New Labour's Britain might have lacked 'sex appeal' or even the 'wow factor' (ugh) had they not been pitched as a guide to the 'new ruins' of Great Britain, despite the PFI-Pseudomodernist structures, rather than wreckages, studied therein. Ruins are sexy, and a recent piece in Vice magazine confirms that young photographers will get more hits and therefore more work by a shoot of an abandoned school or hospital than examples of an impoverished community working together to reclaim a sense of 'place'.[251] In the particular case of hauntology, the description of these lost times or lost futures connect one's passivised/pacified disenfranchisement and alienation to a very remote possibility of utopia, albeit one that's been lost. Foucault's description of 'heterotopias' applies to lost futures: heterotopias, meaning other-places, exist not just beyond our usual conceptions of space, but they also subvert the possibilities of language or images to reduce them to comprehension. They operate through their own meanings, which one can offer fidelity to by researching and listening closely. Foucault describes heterotopias as places that are 'disturbing' and disrupt language; where, like K.'s paralysis and fatigue when approaching a decisive official or access to the Castle, syntax itself is unravelled:

> heterotopias desiccate speech, stop words in their tracks, contest the very possibility of language at its source; they dissolve our myths and sterilize the lyricism of our sentences.[252]

These non-times and lost futures in the music of Burial or imagery of Oldfield Ford signals also a means of imagining an alternative future. A public defence of basic housing, healthcare, working rights and a more equal and just society will require a class-consciousness, of working-class populations across Europe, America and the world realising their common economic position and possibilities of organising together to defend their interests. Such a class-consciousness should reclaim then what are not ruins but working-class neighbourhoods, often multiracial and populated places (faces and figures have been often cropped out of ruinporn photos in exchange for old wheel-chairs and melancholy graffiti).[253] Against the catastrophe and negation, it is the people within non-places and impoverished communities across London, across the UK, that must map their communities and assert who they are. Their 'ruination' is caused by specific political and economic imperatives. Rather than feeling a voyeuristic arousal or catholic shame at the ruins of the non-place, there is a more pragmatic solution to the problem of ruinporn. If the problem is the negation of community and political agency, then rather than clicking through another Flickr stream of totally bodacious 'Urbex' photography, one might instead walk into these communities and help articulate the voices one find. Social democracy as a call to arms can find its way in articulating these voices, documenting these real processes of 'ruination', providing effective community advocacy and engaging in real qualitative study of what makes a 'place', even in a 'non-place': how communities are quickly formed and come together. Bringing together democratic communities will always be one of the most obvious bulwarks of resistance to neoliberal capitalism: a time-demanding and often ineffective resistance, but by far more sincere than acts of targeted violence, hacking or high-brow critique. Working-class communities do not need a new left-wing middle-class missionary movement. But effective progress could be made in bringing out the stories and voices of marginal and marginalised communities, especially sites faced with demolition, discrimination or closure. Martin Parr's photography has brilliantly demonstrated the way in which casual middle-class British life can make for excellent and darkly humorous aesthetic spectacle. Where is its contemporary urban working-class equivalent?

Finally, there is a danger in completely dismissing the ruin. Surely the attractions of the Athenian ruin or the wrecked Iron Age fort are well beyond the scope of neoliberal capitalism? Whilst wandering amongst the overgrown grasses, lost symbols and crumbled brick of an unknowable civilisation from the past, one is also reminded that humanity too is a product of nature, its former grandeur now claimed only by the more resilient flora and fauna, that long after the death of the last woman or man will live on other living natural forces. Georg Simmel best articulates this doubt: 'it is the fascination of the ruin that here the work of man appears to us entirely as a product of nature'.254 But the ultimate difference in hauntology, ruinporn and a contempt of non-places is a fascination not with the powers of 'Nature', but with the powers of neoliberal capitalism, that through some faraway financial transaction, chief executive decision or property-owner's scheme these great structures of our lives are closed, terminated, boarded-up. The contemporary fascination with retro cultures and new ruins betrays a quietism that passively submits in awe to its own negation by neoliberal capitalism. The Urbex visionaries have the courage to climb into these ruins and take beautiful photographs of nature regaining a foothold over former sites of civilisation: fine, but it leaves the average person with a false idea that social change can only arrive via hurricane, tsunami, zombie apocalypse or catastrophe that sweeps capitalist civilisation away, leaving a plucky band of survivors to start off on a clean slate, and not instead through a revolution or popular progressive social democratic movement that workers establish and organise. The problem of negated time and space, on both individual and social dimensions, requires a more vicious, intelligent and optimistic approach.

9

The Drowned and the Saved

Power exists in all the varieties of the human social organisation, more or less controlled, usurped, conferred from above
or recognised from below, assigned by merit, corporate
solidarity, blood, or position: it is likely that a certain degree
of man's domination over man is inscribed in our genetic
patrimony as gregarious animals. It is not proved that power
is intrinsically harmful to the collectivity. – Primo Levi, *The
Drowned and the Saved* [255]

When did 'us' – what Levi calls the 'collectivity', we ourselves –
become the source of our own problems? Was it when we realised
that one could board an overcrowded public train quicker if one
mapped where exactly the doors stopped, and stood in the same
place for five minutes in preparation? How did the aggressive
idiocy of Jeremy Clarkson come to delight so many? At what
point did the collectivity realise that it was quicker just not to
queue, but push, pressure, complain? Or that it was okay every
now and then to be horrible to other people, to make jokes about
'do-gooders' or being nice, so that children were brought up to
vilify the weak rather than try to help them?

It is time to step outside the traditional façade of the distant,
omniscient author and discuss my own doubts and experiences
and how they inform this book. One's life experience informs
one's intellectual position far more than whatever obtuse or
abstract theory gets quoted or edited out of the overall narrative.
Primo Levi's testimony of his survival of Auschwitz is a
companion that'll introduce a discussion of ethics, fascism and
the danger of collapsing before religious idols or powerful ideas.
All this forms the basis for the claims of the conclusion about the

necessity for social democracy, law, and constitution.

The arguments in *Negative Capitalism* are in danger of flopping in their occasional reliance on vague and unquantifiable abstractions to describe social facts. Power is described as an external force, one that does not display physical marks of existence, like the material elements of the periodic table, but one that is outside in an immaterial way, in the sense of rhythm or potential. Power describes the tension of relations in general society, a tension which continually operates and which cannot possibly disappear – the non-hierarchical would be a tyranny of consensus. Power's object is the consent of general life to agree without opposition to its operation. Negation is cynical consent. This new language of describing the contemporary era is necessarily theoretical, using new ideas to describe new sensations. It is a highly abstract description of vicious social facts, sacrificing specificity for concision, but vague theorising is an irritating tendency found in most contemporary theoretical analysis, ruining the work of most academics, even the few with good intentions. Why can't things or facts be described in their own terms, as they actually are? Perhaps not being able to experience the world except through an interface mechanism like a screen, theory, story, soundtrack or competitive interactive function is a definition of being modern. No one can say – and tangled somewhere in that final statement is the riddle of the cynicism and uncertainties of the neoliberal era. No-one can say, but everyone's saying something. The banality of modern communication.

Strange how certain songs or phrases from poems or films stay in the imagination long after the fact, making themselves heard in one's day-dreams, often containing some subconscious message expressed as internal mental noise. The words of Kafka, Levi, and Dostoevsky are like that for me, and have given me the inspiration at times to stand up and take responsibility for what I see and desire. Levi increasingly repeats his vocation to act as a 'witness', to report the events he saw as faithfully as he could, despite the impossibility of being a true witness like those who saw the gorgon truly, the depths of violence in the Nazi death camps, the drowned, of which Levi is offering testimony through his own experiences.[256] The witness has an ethical responsibility to reporting and remembering the event, of speaking the truth despite the force of violence inflicted against them. This is, intellectually at least, the opposite of fascism, which operates on manipulating the democratic body by using fears and uncertainties to wrench out hate, a power which both excites and makes one ever more cowardly. The depression and disenchantment of language by contemporary politicians into charmless and vacant nonsense, or the increasing desires for violent responses to rioters by the police and Home Office, all suggest a resurgent desire for fascist authority around the cult of national pride and the fear of further material deprivation, usually blamed on jihadi terrorists or non-white immigrants.[257]

Unlike previous eras such as the 1960s or 1980s, an entrenched cynicism will make building a progressive social democratic movement capable of beating fascism difficult, without further alienating the working class from politics. The politics of guilt leads to righteousness, which is ultimately a conservative and priggish position. But desire and optimism are real, and can resist fascism in acting against the grain and gambling despite the worst odds. Hence the inspiring importance still sometimes heard for a resistance to capitalism based on love or *agape* – a universal love for all beings. These are beautiful and profoundly moral, and therefore suspicious ideas, unable to effect anything except accelerated righteousness on those that possess them. But the feeling of creative and shared desire is one emotional and physical start-point of a resistance to despair and fascism, passions felt momentarily but difficult to forget, like on a rare night off with a friend or lover, in the middle of a riot or a fight where – at last! – one throws the punch back, proudly refusing the righteous arrogance of being a passive victim.

Fascism offers pathetic consolation to the victims, the silent, to those who abdicate in cowardice their own responsibility to truth, to the equality and civility necessary for stable societies. Levi called it a 'willed ignorance' – throughout the *Drowned and Saved* he uncomfortably waivers between trying not to judge the Germans, those who exterminated his people in the death camps and attempted to exterminate him, and trying to understand how the ordinary mass of German people allowed fascism to exist in power for twelve years.[258] Of course the Germans were effected by a particular cowardice in not confronting anti-Semitism at its earliest rising points, but Levi describes a certain 'demonism' operating unconsciously throughout all human history and societies where wars and violence horrifically occur.[259] Such events in history are always marked by a cynical complicity in violent orders. This chilling encounter of one of Levi's German correspondents spells out the passivity of fascism, where in a dinner-table conversation regarding recent war crimes trials, a cleaner cynically objects, some twenty years after the end of WW2:

> What could they do about it, our poor soldiers, if they gave them those orders? When my husband came on furlough from Poland, he told me: "Almost all we did was shoot Jews, shoot Jews all the time. My arm hurt from so much shooting." But what was he supposed to do, if they had given him those orders?[260]

There have been innumerable further atrocities since the death-camps, an abyssal amount that no sentence can ever offer meaning to or summarise in a list. These atrocities are committed by ordinary men, as Levi continually reminds one, men with similar faces and backgrounds, similar desires, similar families, friends and pastimes. They passively followed orders: who today if not restricted by the law would also do the same, when it's little more than a case of flicking a gas dial, or buzzing a lethal electric charge at a human guinea pig for answering a question incorrectly, or adjusting the joystick to drop a lethal smart-bomb on an impoverished community in a war that technically doesn't even exist, all because someone in an authority told you to do so? In all cases – Auschwitz, or the Milgram experiment on obedience to authority figures, or modern smart-bomb and drone warfare for young men self-trained on violent video games – young men passively follow orders to commit violent atrocities.[261] The defence of human cooperation and peace against violence needs to begin with a new concept of the common social contract and international legally-binding agreements to prevent violent orders and wars being carried out in the first place. A legal social contract guaranteeing basic human rights, within a constitution that made illegal the possession and even production of all lethal weaponry, might prevent such disasters in the future. Abandoning decision-making to incompetent and corrupt officials in the UK has every time resulted in spectacular misman-agement, inducing a popular cynicism about politicians and therefore surrendering to further incompetent interventions.

This surrender and cynicism has plagued my parents' and their parents' generations. In all cases, simply being against the status quo over unemployment, declining freedoms or abuses was rarely countenanced by being for something. The common response to their riots and protests was "yes, but what do you offer instead?" And the common models of Marx and Lenin on the Left, discredited by history as either irrelevant or intrinsically totalitarian, failed to motivate workers to take charge of their own destinies. Whilst enough has been written about social struggles out on the streets, the primary invasion of neoliberal capital into everyday life took place in legislative regulation. Cynicism and bad strategy hamstrung workers from taking power back during the 1980s as the Thatcher government heavily intervened in working rights trade unions, removing all bases of class solidarity and binding them by ten thousand silken bureaucratic strings.

Each of us faces unemployment, increasing inflation, further poverty and deprivation, cuts to local services, a visible decline in the built environment, so when are the same old lessons of the 1980s learned? The situation today is boringly similar. The rioters in Croydon didn't particularly damage the large shopping malls of Croydon: instead it was parked cars, boarded-up pubs and run-down local shops in West Croydon, the most deprived part of that area, which bore the brunt of the violence. Walking down London Road where much of the violence took place, one sees two tall Ikea chimneys loom over the landscape as landmarks of inaccessible middle-class culture and commodities over a deprived and run-down set of working-class communities. It's a far more simple problem than terms like 'post-capitalism' or zombified Marxist theory indicate, offered by contemporary intellectuals. The question for young people today is how to take responsibility for the future, so that the next generation of young people grow up with a far more effective education with the skills to participate in their communities, take an interest in the world, and look after themselves and those around them with the responsibility, intelligence and compassion that a genuinely democratic and responsible citizenship might expect.

Despair left unchecked can be lethal, and it lends one to ultimately abandon the weight of one's suffering to some convenient and empowering excuse, like belief in a God, or charismatic military leader, or fanatical devotion to a transcendental idea at the expense of human life. Levi is alone here in describing the genuine courage of non-belief, of refusing refuge in idols at one's lowest point. Levi was an Italian Jew but had adopted an informed atheism. Through a mixture of brute luck, a certain opportunism candidly described and privileges earned (he was a trained chemist and multi-lingual), Levi was able to survive in Auschwitz. But by October 1944, filing naked to pass a commission that would decide whether he would continue working or go to the gas chamber, Levi finally felt need to find refuge in prayer:

> For one instant I felt the need to ask for help and asylum; then, despite my anguish, equanimity prevailed: you do not change the rules of the game at the end of the match, nor when you are losing. A prayer under these conditions would have been not only absurd (what rights could I claim? and from whom?) but blasphemous, obscene, laden with the greatest impiety of which a non-believer is capable. I rejected that temptation: I knew that otherwise were I to survive, I would have to be ashamed of it.[262]

Regardless of circumstantial experience, most people will at one point or more fall to such dangerously low depths where belief in a saviour becomes inescapable. There are times where it can become psychologically necessary to externally project internal ideas of goodness or redemption onto an omnipotent being who can carry the suffering individual to a better place. Collective depression, like in the present era, establishes a dangerous vulnerability to powerful ideas that declare their ability to save. Fascism has been particularly popular in making this offer, often in a far more clear language and behaviour of fear and hate than the Left has made. Individually and collectively each of us must challenge and refuse to drown in religious belief or political righteousness. Decisions and ideas must be democratic from their base, and must be informed by open, clear discussion, and a reciprocal good-willed exchange of thought and experience. Fascism worries me. The danger of fascism, like any totalitarian assemblage of power, is the relative ease for it to exist and carry it its atrocities at any point in time:

Few countries can be considered immune to a future tide of violence generated by intolerance, lust for power, economic difficulties, religious or political fanaticism, and racialist attritions. It is therefore necessary to sharpen our senses, distrust the prophets, the enchanters, those who speak and write 'beautiful words' unsupported by intelligent reasons.[263]

I am not comparing the present contemporary situation to the Nazi fascism of the 1930s and 1940s, which would obviously be a crass and historically ignorant move. Instead Levi's words are offered as a bulwark for clear thinking, underlined by a distrust of public relations and unelected powers that determine the conditions of society, and a distrust of the aggressive interventionism and militarism of western states in recent memory. Levi offers hope: war and violence are not inevitable and can be prevented by intelligent and equal discussion. But the majority of people will not create or begin such communities anew, especially when so many aspects of our education, consumer culture and social structures come together to inform 'us' of our powerlessness. To Levi's insight at the beginning can be added: power cannot be intrinsically harmful to the collectivity, because it is possessed by the collectivity. Currently they have abandoned this power to a tiny elite of economic masters and are suffering through their negation and poverty. Using the parlance of the neoliberal era, this sub-contracting of power represents bad value for money. New political collectivities that meet in alternative forums outside of the parliamentary system, with representatives from all communities and sites of employment, could function far better for the health and harmony of all members, and with proper regulation and protection of law, media and politics, some of the rot of corruption can be overcome. Power diffused through its members can neutralise some of the toxicity of tyrannical forces that thrive on negating others, be it through brute force or corrupting their desires through hate and greed.

The excesses and catastrophes of human societies in history are not the responsibility of one psychopathic leader, but by everyone who consents willingly or not to that set of social and economic relations.

The collectivity never made any such decision together. The collectivity has never even had a name or a concept of itself as a democratic body. Attempts have been made to impose a collective and manageable identity from above – the idea of 'Britishness' and defending Britain was very effective in the past at convincing men and women from across colonised parts of the world to abandon their lives for a few inches on the map and someone else's economic interests (and the industrial working-class poor were similarly colonised in terms of their daily lives, social conditions and lack of basic freedoms by industrial capitalism). But Britishness is unravelling in the citizenship tests few subjects of her majesty can answer, in the cynicism popularly felt about wars or the competence of the royal family, and an optimistic Scottish nationalism calling for its own independence.

So when can we trade in exhaustion, depression and poverty for a new model? I'm angry and exhausted by talking, ready to abandon the rot of the old world and its gaffer-tape solutions. Things will worsen, and there's little oxygen left for swimming in the neoliberal shit-stream of excuses and pat cynicism. Collectively, a far more socially sustainable and democratic way must be possible, but can only be made possible by the actions of the collectivity. The question is no longer 'what is to be done?' but 'how?': on the side of progress are the young, the ones who draw on the power of the negative to sweep aside the rules of a game rigged to make a tiny amount of white upper class men very rich. This means 'switching', a sudden turn of crazed anger, rather than wallowing in passive aggression, an effect of not feeling strong enough to talk sincerely. Let's take another way out of the dead-end of history via social democracy, through a new social contract and constitution, citizenship and rights, goals around which movements can easily align and work collectively for, offered to all who will work and embody it. Bound by a responsibility to the future to establish technologically and ecologically sustainable communities that can nourish all.

10

Conclusion: A Politics of the Zoo

Are you a young worker or non-worker today? Then you know already that you have little, and that this little will over time become nothing. You will fight and struggle perhaps with nobility, but this is a debt that is impossible and cannot possibly be repaid. Its demands will keep you numb and negated like the electronically-wired slave you are. There is nothing here, and you yourself feel worthless, negated and, I expect, very angry about this. New weapons are needed to retake history and create a new future, beginning with rage and frustrated intelligence.

The generations of the past have experienced similar hardships. Anger was high then; groups met and discussed their problems, marched peacefully into the streets in the cowed attempt that by amassing together but behaving well and doing nothing, capital would admire the decorum and nobility of the righteous. Cranky voices of the last century have deafened generations with announcements of the imminent end of capitalism. Nothing altered fundamentally, and this anger of today is accompanied by a dangerous cynicism, that if something were to change it would have happened already. I've offered suggestions of how it is to be done because I was sure readers would expect some alternative proposal. A violent and creative revolt that draws on negativity to subvert behaviours and sabotage online networks is one effective starter for disrupting financial capitalism, but overall a sustainable revolt can come only by articulating a common social democracy. To avoid this flopping into the same-old idealism of every other left-wing angry tract, social democracy needs to be guaranteed by specific strategies for a secular constitution, a binding civil law, and a new notion of social democratic citizenship.

Over the next decade the tempo of struggles against financial capitalism will very likely increase. Young people across the world have been negated and disinherited from their public wealth. Whilst smashed up pavement slabs, burning cars and network-hacking make for powerful symbolic weapons, revolt will be thwarted, diverted and defeated if it isn't underpinned by a collective demand for constitutional equal, rights within a federation of socially democratic communities. This isn't a simple return to the state, as *Capitalist Realism* advocated back in 2009, which might lead to a problematic nationalism or worse, well-meaning democrats throwing their lot behind one of the existing discredited British political parties like the Labour party. Social democracy needs to think beyond existing states in order to create a wider universal defence of social life, one that is secular and equal, asserted in plain language by a manifesto and written constitution that could be forged from the coming struggles. Out of the vicious historical clash of dispossessed workers and communities against neoliberal financial capital is a genetic potential that could conceive and produce into being a new, technologically informed, intelligent, compassionate and stable social democracy underpinned by a social contract and secular constitution, ensuring a basic standard of life, access and support for all humans. Life is not an esoteric abstraction but the social relations between you, me and the communities around us. They have the right collectively and democratically to determine their own conditions and decisions, not distant bankers in the Castle of financial capitalism, where every official is awesomely powerful, and no-one at all is accountable, or can give a decisive answer on what the actual economic or social agenda is. There isn't much time – there never is enough time. This isn't melancholia but a call for strategy with a specific goal: transformation of life from an economic politic to a social politic, to a sustainable educated democracy, one that is secular, regulated by a constitution, and technologically progressive.

Against claims that capitalism is nihilistic or self-destructive, what seems like continual crisis is actually a healthy mode of operation that maintains the accumulation of capital by financial elites. The language of crisis and emergency is exploited to maintain and broaden wealth gaps – the term 'austerity' is a convenient excuse for workers to accept declining public services and decreasing wages in terms of the greater economic good. Meanwhile bonuses and private wealth by financiers increases – an effective wealth redistribution from the poor and from what was once held in public to the rich, held in private. Capitalism is doing very well, sucking every minute of life out of me and you in the blind drive for increased productivity and profit. The final report of the High Pay Commission of November 2011, which brought together a fairly neutral and informed sample of representatives from finance, trade unions, politics and journalism, concluded that 'excessive top pay is deeply damaging to the UK as a whole, and urgent action is needed to remedy it'.[264] Its researchers found that the pay of top financial executives has risen in cases by 4000% since 1980 – in the case of Barclays, top pay is now 75 times that of the average employee, compared to a relatively more benign 14.5 times greater difference back in 1979; that the shared GDP of the general workforce has shrunk by 12% over the same period up to 2008, and with recent inflation and frozen wages will have shrunk even further; that over 2010-11 executive pay in the FTSE 100 rose by 49%, compared to a 2.7% rise in the average employee; that whilst in 1979 the top 0.1% of earners took home 1.3% of national income, the top 1% took home 5.9%, and the top 10% took home 28.4% – by 2007 this had increased with the top 0.1% earning 6.5% of national income, the top 1% earning 14.5%, and the top 10% taking home 40% of the national income.[265] The commission ultimately found that 'excessive high pay bears little relation to company success and is rewarding failure'.[266] So if the destructive and negative effects of financial capitalism are so obvious both in one's personal life, and as found in a piece of cohesive national research, how can workers begin to reclaim power?

This is a world without a future: the sense of what if, or the curiosity to map out progress towards a more harmonious future is mostly missing. Futurism today consists of idiotic "Top Ten Must-Have Gadgets!!!!" in a free rag for workers to glance at bleary-eyed on packed-out commuter carriages. Claiming the future requires a strategy. There have been plenty of well-intentioned community activists and democratic groupings which have failed to build a movement that would articulate the demands and desires of a social politic. Where they have failed, the time comes to suggest simple and concrete strategies for which individuals can gather and form communities of creative anger around. There is no *we* or *should* implied here however. I see no sign right now that the future will be reclaimed, or should be, or that effectively the 99% or entirety of humanity will awake out of some black night of irrationality and fulfil their enlightened destinies. It is not from human history but religious idealism that such a hope stems. In arranging and organising all of the ways that neoliberalism damages life individually, psychologically, and socially, negating us into a black hole of exhaustion and poverty, my aim is to provoke a response – how can this be changed?

I suggest my own argument for a creative and passionate social democracy only out of intellectual honesty to readers, who will rightly ask what my alternative is. It brings to mind the pessimistic faith of essayist Michel de Montaigne. Writing at a time of Christian civil war during 16th century France, Montaigne addressed the sceptics of his day with a question that also indicates the limits of cynical resignation in the contemporary neoliberal era. Against the 'dreadful, horrible darkness of irreligion', Montaigne offers: 'If you have anything better, produce it, or submit'.[267] Montaigne's faith in the restrictive certainties of the early modern Christian world have been destroyed by the intellectual movements of enlightenment, founded on a base of mass anger and creative and free innovation, driven by necessity. Enlightenment scepticism threw out the priests, but in the era of industrialised capitalism the merchants crept in and took the reins of power. The transformation is possible, but half-complete. The neoliberal era is profoundly different, and presents far more opportunities for a global social democracy with one major language, and one common awareness of the catastrophic brutality and betrayal of ideologies of the 20th century.

For political conservatives reading this account, arguing for a social democracy like this might seem like children demanding the right to run the school themselves because they understand the needs of children better. It's a humorous image with potentially interesting results, but one that would demonstrate that democratic adults, like children, are unfit to manage their own affairs. With an independent, quality-regulated media; the abolition of MPs and political parties open to lobbying and corruption; improved resources and provision for education and time for self-education; and the forced redistribution of wealth to workers, adults would be capable of taking an interest and consenting to how their communities and workplaces are run. The sorry case of Greece, with austerity measures self-imposed since 2010, demonstrates that social democracy and neoliberal capitalism cannot co-exist without eventual mass debt by the state; and that neoliberal bankers will always ultimately determine government and social conditions until workers violently and collectively resist their intervention. Media reports from Greece, spurious or not, inform Western readers of rising suicide rates, child abandonment, alcoholism and societal fragmentation, all clearly linked to debt and unemployment. The British worker should stop worrying about the size of his or her TV and consider the more terrifying and exciting spectacle of their own uncertain future.

The paperless Castle can be destroyed, whether by the burning torches of its cynical, indebted villagers, or by the self-ruining machinations and disproportionate greed of its sleep-deprived officials. Undermining the castle requires cunning and strategy. Pasquinelli criticises the contemporary anti-capitalist Left for lacking a clear economic strategy, assuming the natural goodness of humanity, and targeting capital at obscure points and not at its heart.[268] The most brilliant contemporary anti-capitalist critics are guilty of assuming that an abstracted multitude, inflated to religious ideal, can through 'love' conquer demonic capital and return to the carefree promised land of the Commons.[269] The actively political Left's failure to articulate a popular or even consistent position stems from its inability to attach itself either to the democratic youth revolts of August 2011, or to the more old-fashioned 'Liberal' position which has historically argued for laissez-faire communitarian policies within a largely social-democratic rubric. Like finance and the disciplines, it too has become rootless and freefloating in a prole-tarianised middle-class precarity, a pacifist arts lecturer's gluten-free grumble. The explanation for this is simple: rendered passive by decades of cynicism and fear, the opposition of the real has been replaced by the meek protest of the symbolic. Such symbolic protest forms like the march, the sit-in or petition have proved themselves ineffective. Marches politely walk themselves away from violent occupations or destructions of meaningful state or commercial properties, never transforming government policy, and resulting in the most dreary moral platitudes concerning righteousness or justice.

Compare these two approaches of complacent cynicism versus passionate negativity as representing two different kinds of contemporary class struggle. Neither one is 'correct' or more valid – the task instead is to harmonise these different reactions into one coherent social democratic drive. The largely middle-class students are in clear contrast to the riots of August 2011, when working-class and 'underclass' youths, alienated, angry and excited by the opportunity, trashed their marginalised communities and smashed up the chainstores which had colonised their local areas into bland clone high-streets. For all the language of freedom and choice in local further education colleges and arts universities in Britain's urban areas, there are now very few opportunities for the young in both cases. Instead, momentarily, these young people felt so pissed off by the lack of any meaningful future or alternatives before them that they took to the streets, set fires burning, laughed and fought policemen transported in from suburban garrisons. The actively political Left has the possibility of generating and leading a wider youth opposition to negative capitalism only by abandoning their moral righteousness and an elitist language for discussing opposition, and fully embracing an optimistic, devious, strategic and techno-logically-informed negativity that makes use of all within it.

Negativity is a very general category for thinking through labour processes and social change. But at any small fault-line like searching for paid work, union disputes, finding an accurate source for information or news, marching to parliament to defend disability welfare benefits or higher education – the wider process of disempowerment is exhibited. One is oppressed by violent police who are institutionally racist and led by corrupt, law-breaking officials; the majority of media is complicit with political policy, from the appointment of Sarah Sands as the new editor of the Evening Standard in March 2012, an ally of Boris Johnson, to News International's unique access to political policy and police information; political representation occurs not in local surgeries but in paid access to government ministers, secured by corporate and financial party funding – in all cases, and there are countless, one rotten interaction loops into a wider process of managed disempowerment, engineering ultimately by the most cynical and debilitating crisis of language. The 'choice' of the customer in education, healthcare or policing, their 'freedom', one apparently offered by 'free markets', has made all real decisions redundant to those who do not possess huge fortunes. Yes, this is all well-known, shit is the same shit. But until now each of us has grouped and worked together in individual struggles; we've talked rather than acted; and we've abandoned the arguments for civil law and constitution that might empower language to once again describe and defend not just individual human rights, but collective social rights. And we've assumed the dream-state of the consumer-individual, allowing the politics of identity, freedom and choices to blur the more fundamental processes of negation. The collective process of disempowerment was overlooked, for which no single political march or local election can singularly influence. The language of historical materalism can no longer effect if either, when the validity and usage of language itself is at stake. This book comes almost too late for words, but not too late for strategy. Neither freedom nor happiness (as commonly understood) are healthy end-states for a social democracy, but a harmonious, sustainable, merit-determined and educated community of equal agents who act as a whole through agreement, not consensus.

Observable on the 2011 Higher Education protests in London was a self-kettling, a kettled mindset, as demonstrators behaved as if they were already trapped and had lost, and therefore retreated into predictable and trapped confrontations with the immediate figures of oppression, disorderly policemen, rather than the sources of oppression, banks and corrupt political institutions. Negativity is sustained by cowed consent, and directly violating the means of control, identified in this book, will be hard, desperate, sometimes isolating, near-impossible. But the glittering prize is there: a basic quality of life and wellbeing collectively determined by a new law and constitution, bringing closure on such submission to the economic politic of neoliberalism. So, in keeping with a trend in contemporary left-leaning cultural studies polemics, let's draw this account to a close with a rallying quotation against political tyranny by Spinoza:

> for no one is able to transfer to another his natural right or faculty to reason freely and to form his own judgement on any matters whatsoever, nor can he be compelled to do so. Consequently, a government that attempts to control men's minds is regarded as tyrannical, and a sovereign is thought to wrong his subjects and infringe their right when he seeks to prescribe for every man what he should accept as true and reject as false, and what are the beliefs that will inspire him with devotion to God. All these are matters belonging to individual right, which no man can surrender even if he should wish.[270]

I have one problem with this kind of argument however: it's easy to slide into the same passive and sympathetic celebration of individual liberty, borrowing the words of another era when such a struggle was so counter-politically loaded. The problem each of us faces is that social life is not just made up of men, nor is it purely human (what of the animal, the cyborg, the bacterial?); without being bathetic, one lesson of the atrocities of the 20th century is that there are no inviolable natural or innate humans rights that will universally protect humanity. The above sentiment would find David Cameron and Noam Chomsky in agreement. Against Spinoza and his repeaters, passively exhorting and defending an abstract libertarian ideal of freedom always returns us back to the individual and his false set of choices, the apparent exercise of such freedom. Negative capitalism disempowers us not individually, but collectively. Collective rights must be determined and must be acted from nothing, through word, law and actions.

Explaining why one *should* feel angry can have a contrary effect. Our lives are determined by our actions collectively, and I hope only to have identified weak points and new strategies in a struggle for a basic standard of living without anxiety, debt, precarious work and poverty, beyond a culture where the future and the present have been colonised by financial imperatives. Anonymous hacking missions, community 'supermarket sweep' smash-and-grab events, and strategic acts of violence against key sites of negative capitalism would energise a wider movement of real opposition rather than symbolic protest. Internet networks and servers could be targeted in revenge for the continuous intervention of surveillance imposed by these organisations on workers' lives. Or – and I articulate this position only for vicious irony – aghast at the prospect of beastly violence, the Left might instead re-engage with its middle-class mothership of tepid Liberalism, asserting the values of the family, rights for minorities (except equal employment, incarceration or police stop-and-search levels – imagine if white middle class citizens submitted themselves to this kind of parity of esteem?) and the like. Although a fundamentally hypocritical and complacent position, it would be more intellectually honest than attempting to foment the end of capitalism via e-petition or a paranoid litter-free protest camp outside a major London tourist attraction.

Seems laughable, but the above is the fundamental impli-cation of those who believe change begins and ends every five years at the ballot box. Instead an embodied resistance is needed, distinct in its creative destruction, one that hacks and physically disrupts the essential infrastructure of negative capitalism – financial exchanges, media outlets, and corporate headquarters. Bartleby's 'I would prefer not to' becomes an expression of the most fatalistic and idiotic passivity that the Left must abandon with sustained and vicious humour.[271] Bartleby can prefer for as long as he likes: I will not. Such an optimistic violence becomes creative, sovereign and 'law-making' in its sheer urgency, as Walter Benjamin put it.[272] The violent and animalistic multitude must hack into financial algorithms and spread PR disinformation via the news-wires, whilst at the same time organising sustained looting and coordinated occupations of financial and governmental centres.

This enthusiastic if belligerent conclusion so far stumbles into a few dangers, as Kafka would remind. The villagers of the Castle enjoy the security of their positions, their freedom to live and the comfortable gains of hard-won status and employment. Widespread Left-wing revolt against negative capitalism has largely failed because it has lacked a democratic base, with instead an encroaching far-Right politics of religious or political nationalism infusing oppressed communities across the globe. Such a violence would instead play into the hands of fascism and bored opportunism, and reinforce calls by voter-consumers for greater security and policing. Resisting negative capitalism requires a rationale, and not merely a suggestion that, 150 years on, Marx was indeed right after all. This is small consolation to a system that does not concern right or good or truth, and which is increasingly organising all life into regimes of abstracted continuous productivity and financial debt value. Lastly, advocating violence is also a little disingenuous: if it's such a good strategy, why am I explaining this instead of just going ahead and carrying out propaganda of the deed? Because, ultimately, violence alone does not convince me.

Recall for a moment Primo Levi's refusal of prayer in the last chapter. I am confronted by a system that denies truth and is founded on deceptive information, be it in cynical media or the shifting values of goods traded as capital. Neoliberal capitalism is the basis of a global arrangement of exchange that will damage the planet and lead to profound suffering and death of all life. Truth is not just an ethical privilege or right, but also a duty – as democratic agents you and I embody a truth. Ethically, the experiences, desires, rights and livelihoods of each person in common are our truth, one that cannot just be defended but must be asserted. What if, politically or socially, I got what I wanted? If after a protest or campaign the world transformed as I had called for? I would need to be sure then that I had thought through exactly the kind of society I wanted to live and work in, and that I had committed my time most effectively and most strategically to attaining this goal. This potential seems awesome, unrealistic: for so long each movement has failed or been thwarted, therefore nothing can succeed. Indulging in pessimism leads to inaction. When truth is demanded at once by a force larger than any known army, beyond the scope of any military drone or mercenary militia, it will be proof that humans can act in their own interests, overcoming the restrictive Castle walls of fear, cynicism and repressive morality.

An effective and constitutional assertion of human rights, of free time, of public space, basic working conditions, might convert into meaningful democratic political currency for which an empowered global proletariat might begin to assert their interests against neoliberal capital. A move of no confidence in the UK Parliament might begin from an online campaign, establishing a new national parliament with an agreement by referenda on the contents of a secular, republican constitution that guarantees democratic rights, a new standard of education, healthcare and employment access, equal legal rights, and the establishment of an independent and responsibly-regulated mass media. An international movement of workers against military states like the US and China might force the UN, anxious to manage a global movement of impassioned social democratic currents, to enact taxes on financial exchange, restrictions on protectionism and financial speculation, and install a global and internationally legally-binding social contract with access to shelter, clean water and food, and the global redistribution of wealth from abstracted capital into expenditure on infrastructure, healthcare, and into the wages of workers.

Alongside a more abstract law-making violence, negative capitalism can be limited and itself restrained by a democratic and constitutional defence of the public. This requires global and local agreements on working hours and basic wages; on closure of tax-loopholes, and the introduction of a Tobin tax on currency exchanges to prevent parasitic financial speculation; fixed and legally-binding restrictions on carbon emissions amongst all states, on access to shelter, drinkable water, birth control. It would require a return to a Bretton Woods-style fixed currency equilibrium, thereby preventing economic protectionism via increasing taxations on imports or flooding rival economies with cheap exports, as is the case currently. In the UK, it would mean becoming a secular and constitutional federation of states, using closed corporate tax loopholes and forcible wealth redistribution to fund the development of new high-tech industries dependent on domestic manufacturing, guaranteeing full regulated employment and sustainable self-sufficiency. On an individual plane, it calls for a 'free uncooperation' as Pasquinelli has it, or better yet, a 'conscious inertia' as Dostoevsky's Underground Man announced earlier, resisting the intense productivity-drives of capital with a cheeky laziness that proudly refuses to work.[273] Some people will already know what I mean and will laugh. But for the workaholics and the long downtrodden, free uncooper- ation is a tart and proud tonic.

The collectivity is responsible for its own historical progress. It possesses its own power, life: that which capital requires to exploit for its operation, something which it abstracts and negates into privatised profiteering. Life needs strategic aims to articulate a new sustainable future for itself: simply being for better regulated banks or against the extinction of polar bears doesn't cut it. It requires strategic aims in common that are open to all and specific: equal human rights for all nationally and inter- nationally, in one social contract that confers citizenship. This citizenship expects in turn ethical responsibilities as part of the contract – to observe law, participate in communities, create and observe intelligent compassion for all beings, in exchange for access to shelter, resources, a basic global wage and educational standard, employment and healthcare. It could be paid for by an international redistribution of wealth to democratic communities of workers, administered by a new United Nations-style body, where all states have equal representation, without vetoes. This couldn't be gently or rationally reorganised, but like the end of the Christian Church's power-hold over Europe, it could occur by the negative, creative and vicious strategy of a deviously progressive and democratic collectivity against financial capital. The basic tenet of financial capitalism – the right of a tiny elite to extract profit from labour and retain this profit for the idiotic propagation of their own status and individual power – can be overcome as the hubris of another age, rendered illegal, irrational and obscene.

The collectivity need a new common agreement, therefore radicalised communists, social democrats and others must come and present their arguments and ideas in a clear, public and strategic matter for democratic debate. Whether this is formed into an international movement before or after serious collapse remains to be seen. In effect these demands are fundamentally biopolitical, regarding the protection and support of human life by the *polis*, a return to a socialised politic. But in the economic politic of negative capitalism, capital has pervaded almost all aspects of life, leading ultimately to a 'thanatopolitics' of mass starvation, abstraction of life into dividualised data, and social collapse, as self-seeking Western entrepreneurs use bowdlerised survival-of-the-fittest ideas to justify their expropriation of common wealth through private profit.[274]

Again it must be stated: being simply *for* or *against* capitalism is a dead-end of melancholic passivity, popular with lazy academics, activists and artists who consider themselves as the only valid opposition in town. Moral categories of righteousness, or indignation, are entirely irrelevant to its processes. Negation is a condition of disempowerment in an era determined by financial capitalism, where neoliberalism is its theorist, advocate and apologist, and cynicism its most common collective response. Whatever the continued economic crises in Europe and the US, financial capitalists will continue to increase their profits and share of wealth production, and the token punishment of one or two 'rogue' speculators whitewashes the wider process of upwards wealth redistribution. Life is too short to waste time in symbolic struggles like e-petitions, marches, or the first-past-the-post electoral system, and these processes and the sources of information used to form public opinion are largely manipulated and forged anyway. Thanatopolitics must be met with a politics of the zoo. If anxiety is an omnipresent fear of unknown cause, then it is clear how and why negative capitalism pervades life and is the cause of this anxiety. It is the fearful villagers, and not the anxious K., who alone have the potential to destroy the castle, in a violent anonymous revolt which destroys financial and information control architectures. If the Castle is to be undermined with cunning and strategy, workers must realise the desperation of a lost future quickly and act optimistically, intelligently, collectively and with devious negativity towards the embodied destruction of the old Castle around them.

Endnotes

1   Mark Fisher, Capitalist Realism: is there no alternative? (Ropley: Zero, 2009), 83.

2   World Health Authority, "SUPRE the WHO Worldwide Initiative for the Prevention of Suicide" [www.who.int /mental_health/management/en/SUPRE_flyer1.pdf – URL last accessed 31/03/12].

3   Source: Deaths Registrations Data, Office for National Statistics. Deaths by specified cause in London, 2010. Data requested. Young men refers to all males aged 15-34. The number of deaths by land traffic accident in the same age-group totalled 56, and for violent assaults 59.

4   Conversation overheard by Walter Benjamin, "Franz Kafka", Illuminations, ed. Hannah Arendt, trans. Harry Zorn (London: Pimlico, 1999), 112-113.

5   The UK population in the year leading up the mid-2010 stood at 62.3 million. At the last UK election of 2010, the total electorate numbered around 47 million. Of these, 65% turned out to vote – a figure of around 30.5 million. Of this 30.5 million, 36% voted Conservative, the eventual minority government which ended up forming a coalition with the Lib Dems which they have since dominated, and of which the Lib Dems subsequently abandoned the majority of their manifesto pledges and policies to adopt a neoliberal Conservative agenda. 36% of 30.5 million is about 11 million, the number who have ultimately democratically elected the government, against 36 million who did not – 23% of the UK electorate, or 18% of the UK population. See BBC News, "General Election 2010 Key Stories" for an overview [http://news.bbc.co.uk/1/hi/8666221.stm].

6   "Before the Law". Franz Kafka, The Trial, in The Complete Novels: The Trial, America, The Castle, trans. Willa and

Edwin Muir (London: Vintage, 2008), 185.

7 Gilles Deleuze, "Postscript on Control Societies", in Negotiations 1972-1990, trans. Martin Joughin (New York: Columbia University Press, 1995), 182. Text originally appeared in May 1990 in L'autre Journal 1.

8 Deleuze, "Postscript", Negotiations, 181-2.

9 For a somewhat deceptive introduction to this, see Michel Foucault, Birth of Biopolitics: Lectures at the Collège de France 1978-79, ed. Michel Senellart; trans. Graham Burchell (Basingstoke: Palgrave Macmillan, 2008), 21-22.

10 Michel Foucault, Discipline and Punish. The Birth of the Prison, trans. Alan Sheridan (New York: Vintage second edition, 1995), 26; see also 19, 23, 25-28, 102, 136-160, 141, 171, 183-184 , 308.

11 Foucault, Discipline and Punish, 137.

12 Foucault, Discipline and Punish, 136-160, 141, 171, 183-184; Deleuze, "Postscript", Negotiations, 178-179.

13 Deleuze, "Postscript", Negotiations, 178.

14 Using the term by Foucault, Discipline and Punish, 98-99.

15 Deleuze, "Postscript", Negotiations, 182.

16 Renato Curcio and Alberto Franceshini, in a supplement to Corrispondenza internazionale, 1982 – cit. in Tiqqun, This Is Not a Program, trans. Joshua David Jordan (Los Angeles: Semiotext(e): 2011), 49.

17 Herbert Marcuse, One-Dimensional Man. Studies in the Ideology of Advanced Industrial Society (Abingdon; New York: Routledge Classics, 2007); Nina Power, One Dimensional Woman (Ropley: Zero, 2009).

18 Deleuze, "Postscript", Negotiations, 180.

19 William S. Burroughs, The Soft Machine (New York: Grove Press, 1992), 90.

20 Deleuze, "Postscript", Negotiations, 181.

21 Foucault, Discipline and Punish, 106, 113, 121-124, 130, 143, 170-176, 205, 240-244, 269.

22 Foucault, Discipline and Punish, 9.

23 For a somewhat deceptive introduction to this, see Foucault, Birth of Biopolitics, 21-22.

24 Foucault, Discipline and Punish,10.

25 Foucault, Discipline and Punish, 26; see also 19, 23, 25-28, 102, 308.

26 Deleuze, Foucault, trans. Seán Hand (Minneapolis: University of Minnesota Press, 1988), 92.

27 Paolo Virno, A Grammar of the Multitude. For an Analysis of Contemporary Forms of Life, trans. Isabella Bertoletti, James Cascaito, Andrea Casson (New York; Los Angeles: Semiotext(e), 2004), 81.

28 Virno, Grammar of the Multitude, 83.

29 Franco "Bifo" Berardi, The Soul at Work: From Alienation to Autonomy, trans. Francesca Cadel and Giuseppina Mecchia (Los Angeles: Semiotext(e), 2009), 21-22, 87, 131, 188, 200.

30 Berardi, Precarious Rhapsody. Semiocapitalism and the pathologies of the post-alpha generation, ed. Erik Empson and Stevphen Shukaitis; trans. Arianna Bove, Erik Empson, Michael Goddard, Guiseppina Mecchia, Antonella Schintu, and Steve Wright (London: Minor Compositions, 2009), 94-95.

31 Berardi, Precarious Rhapsody, 55; the 'catastrophic' in Jean Baudrillard, "Symbolic Exchange and Death", 123-124; "Fatal Strategies", 193-201, in Selected Writings, ed. Mark Poster and trans. Jacques Mourrain et al. (Palo Alto: University of Stanford Press, 1988); Dimitris Papadopoulos, Niamh Stephenson and Vassilis Tsianos, Escape Routes: Control and Subversion in the Twenty-first Century (London; Ann Arbor, MI: Pluto, 2008), xiii, xx.

32 Giorgio Agamben, Homo Sacer. Sovereign Power and Bare Life, trans. Daniel Heller-Roazen (Stanford: Stanford University Press, 1998), 9.

33 Michael Hardt and Antonio Negri, Empire (Cambridge,

MA: Harvard University Press, 2001), 24.

34 Alexander R. Galloway and Eugene Thacker, The Exploit: A Theory of Networks (London; Minneapolis: University of Minnesota Press, 2007), 79; Hardt and Negri, Empire, 357. See also Hardt and Negri, Multitude: War and Democracy in the Age of Empire (New York: Penguin Press, 2004), 358.

35 Galloway and Thacker, The Exploit, 101.

36 Biocapitalism comes from Vanni Codeluppi, but its clearest proponent is Christian Marazzi in The Violence of Financial Capitalism, trans. Kristina Lebedeva & Jason Francis Mc Gimsey (Los Angeles: Semiotext(e), 2011), 49.

37 Marazzi, Violence of Financial Capitalism, 54-55.

38 Virno, Grammar of the Multitude, 52, 55-58, 61, 68, 71, 90.

39 Marazzi, Violence of Financial Capitalism, 49; Matteo Pasquinelli, Animal Spirits: A Bestiary of the Commons (Rotterdam: NAi Publishers, 2008), 29, 98-115.

40 Marazzi, Violence of Financial Capitalism, 55; see also 57, 73-74 on this.

41 Karl Marx, "Fragment on Machines", Grundrisse, trans. Martin Nicolaus (London: Penguin, 1973), 693. On general intellect, see Virno, Grammar of the Multitude, 40-42, 63-65, 68-71, 105-111; Pasquinelli, Animal Spirits, 107; Marazzi, Violence of Financial Capitalism, 113; Berardi, Precarious Rhapsody, 71; Hardt and Negri, Empire, 29.

42 Marx, Economic and Philosophic Manuscripts of 1844, cit. in Marazzi, Violence of Financial Capitalism, 116.

43 Pasquinelli, Animal Spirits, 13, 16, 154.

44 Specifically this criticism refers to Tiqqun, This is Not a Program, 66, 71; Berardi, Soul at Work, 78, 81, 220; Papadopoulos et al., Escape Routes, xvi-xx, 235; Agamben, Homo Sacer, 12-14, 102.

45 Pasquinelli, Animal Spirits, 27, 35, 51.

46 Pasquinelli, Animal Spirits, 34.

47 Deleuze, "Postscript", Negotiations, 182.

48 Slavoj Žižek, The Ticklish Subject: The Absent Centre of Political Ontology (London; New York: Verso, 2000), 184.

49 See Foucault, Birth of Biopolitics, 79-81, 116-120.

50 See "Postface: Defining Neoliberalism", in Philip Mirowski and Dieter Plehwe (eds.), The Road from Mont Pèlerin: The Making of the Neoliberal Thought Collective (Cambridge, MA: Harvard University Press, 2009), 433-444.

51 David Harvey's term: see A Brief History of Neoliberalism (New York: Oxford University Press, 2005), 8, 19, 31-33.

52 Harvey, Brief History of Neoliberalism, 1-2.

53 Harvey, Brief History, 29, 73, 160.

54 Refer also to Harvey's previous The Condition of Postmodernity. An Enquiry into the Origins of Cultural Change (Cambridge, MA: Blackwell, 1992), 137, 141-145.

55 Manuel Castells, The Rise of the Network Society.(Second Edition). Volume I of The Information Age trilogy (Chichester: Wiley-Blackwell, 2010), 465-470. On Harvey's notion of 'flexible accumulation', see Harvey, Condition of Postmodernity, 124, 189-196.

56 Both Paul Bremer, head of the Coalition Provisional Authority in Iraq, and Ludwig Erhard, head of the economic administration of the Anglo-American zone, removed price controls and all financial regulations, founding the happiness of the state on economic freedom: see Foucault, Birth of Biopolitics, 80-81; Harvey, Brief History, 5.

57 Foucault, Birth of Biopolitics, 1-2, 15.

58 Marazzi, Violence of Financial Capitalism, 109-110; Virno, Grammar of the Multitude, 110-111.

59 See on this Sukhdev Sandhu's excellent Night Haunts (London: Artangel/Verso, 2007).

60 Container ships were too large for the London docks, and from 1963 onwards a new container dock was built at Tilbury in Essex. See Fiona Rule, London Docklands: A History of the Lost Quarter (Hersham: Ian Allan, 2009), 267-

269.

61 Rule, London Docklands, 269. By 1981 the last of the east London docks at West India, Millwall and the "Royals" at Silvertown had closed.

62 See Peter Clarke's Hope and Glory: Britain 1900-1990 (London: Penguin, 1997), 357.

63 Thatcher also notoriously claimed in an ITV World in Action interview on 14 January 1978 that 'People are really rather afraid that this country might be swamped by people with a different culture', setting another unfortunately popular precedent in British politics – xenophobia and racism. For further discussion of race in the UK, see Paul Gilroy, 'There Ain't No Black in the Union Jack': The cultural politics of race and nation (London: Hutchinson, 1987), 43-59, 68-69.

64 Thatcher quoted in Joe Kerr and Andrew Gibson (eds.), London from Punk to Blair (London: Reaktion, 2003), 10.

65 See Clarke, Hope and Glory: Britain 1900-1990, 213-223, 255; Roy Porter, London: A Social History (London: Penguin, 2000), 427-431, 438-441.

66 Whilst leading progressives within the post-war governments like William Beveridge and Aneurin Bevan worked to create a 'new society' with equal opportunities for all, Conservative opposition and a heavily-depleted post-war economy forced much of this reconstruction to be delivered as cheaply as possible.

67 Owen Hatherley, Militant Modernism (Winchester: Zero Books, 2008), 8-10, 40-42.

68 Colin Jones and Alan Murie, The Right to Buy. Analysis & Evaluation of a Housing Policy (Real Estate Issues) (Oxford: Blackwell, 2006), 28-31.

69 Andy Merrifield found that since 1985 over 74,000 public sector units had been lost. See Merrifield, "Flexible Marxism and the Metropolis", in A Companion to the City, ed. Gary Bridge and Sophie Watson (Oxford: Blackwell, 2003), 132.

See also Peter Clarke, Hope and Glory: Britain 1900-1990, 381-383, 396.

70   Roy Porter provides numerous statistics of the bleak situation of London in the early 1990s – 20% unemployment in Hackney and Haringey, 35% in Kings Cross; homelessness increasing from 16,579 in 1980 (an already high figure given the near-eradication of homelessness during the 1950s and 1960s) to 65,000 single people and 37,740 households. One 1991 survey found that 48% of people surveyed wanted to leave London. See Porter, London: A Social History, 445, 453-457.

71   This tendency towards turning culture and heritage into a commodity began with the Civic Amenities Act 1967, which allowed local councils to establish heritage conservation areas – by the mid-1980s there were nearly 30,000 listed buildings and over 300 conservation areas - see Porter, London: A Social History, 450.

72   Michael Heseltine, speaking on the Docklands in 1981, quoted in Kerr and Gibson (eds.), London from Punk to Blair, 10.

73   Heseltine later wrote this in his published memoirs. Quoted in Rule, London's Docklands, 271.

74   See Porter, London: A Social History, 460-464.

75   Harvey, "The Urban Process Under Capitalism: A Framework for Analysis", reproduced in The Blackwell City Reader, ed. Bridge and Watson, 116-117.

76   BNP candidate Derek Beackon was elected councillor for the Millwall ward in September 1993 – see Porter, London: A Social History, 466-467. Despite the huge level of construction and new jobs in the London Docklands, unemployment for local people was only reduced by 2.8% to 11.2% – Rule, London's Docklands, 275.

77   On Soja's metropolarities, see "Six Discourses on the Postmetropolis", reproduced in The Blackwell City Reader

ed. Bridge and Watson, 192-194. Polarities are marked not just by class but also race: institutional racism and violence against male black youth has been a continual feature of the Metropolitan police from the Mangrove Trial of 1970 in Notting Hill to Operation Swamp 81 and the Brixton race-related riots of 1981, 1985 and later 1995, to the failure to prosecute all the murderers of Stephen Lawrence and continual over-targeting of black male youths for random stop and searches (although increasingly working-class Asian male youths are being over-targeted in proportion to white males). The London Plan, using statistics gathered in 2006-7 before the most recent economic downturn, found that London contained the highest UK unemployment rate, 7.2%. Of this average figure it found that the black and ethnic minority unemployment figure stood at 11.7%, whilst that of white Londoners stood at less than half, 5.4%. See Greater London Authority, The London Plan: Spatial Development Strategy for Greater London. Consolidated with Alterations since 2004 (London: Greater London Authority, February 2008), 35.

78 See Genevieve Roberts and Jonathan Prynn, "The Dispossessed: Eight out of ten children live in poverty in three areas of city", The Evening Standard 19 July 2010. Note also the Greater London Authority's 2008 London Plan put the figure of 'income poverty' at 52% in Inner London and 39% in Greater London, the highest rate of poverty overall in Britain – see Greater London Authority, London Plan, 35.

79 Fredric Jameson, Postmodernism, Or, the Cultural Logic of Late Capitalism (New York: Verso, 1992) 5-6, 10.

80 Report carried out by the National Centre for Social Research – see Alison Park et al., British Social Attitudes 2010-11: Exploring Labour's Legacy – The 27th Report, chapter one, p2. See also the most recent 28th report.

81 See The Guardian and the London School of Economics,

Reading the Riots: Investigating England's Summer of Disorder, pub. 14 December 2011.

82 Doreen Massey, writing in 1994, in Space, Place and Gender (Minneapolis: University of Minnesota Press, 2001), 163.

83 Foucault, Birth of Biopolitics, 147, 226, 269, 278.

84 Indicated by Gary Becker's pioneering work, Human Capital, 1964; see also Theodor Schultz, Investing in Human Capital, 1971.

85 Deleuze, "Postscript", Negotiations, 181.

86 Foucault, Birth of Biopolitics, 57-67; Deleuze, "Postscript", Negotiations, 179-180.

87 Steven R. Shaviro, "The 'Bitter Necessity' of Debt: Neoliberal Finance and the Society of Control", Paper presented at Debt Conference April 29-May 1 2010, University of Wisconsin-Milwaukee, 8-9.

88 The High Pay Commission, Director's Pensions: in it for themselves? (London: High Pay Commission, 2011), 4-7; High Pay Commission, More for Less: what has happened to pay at the top and does it matter? (London: High Pay Commission, 2011), 5-9; Wenchao Jin, Robert Joyce, David Phillips and Luke Sibieta, Poverty and Inequality in the UK: 2011. IFS Commentary C118 (London: Institute for Fiscal Studies, 2011), 1-3.

89 Marazzi, Violence, 33-37, 40-42.

90 Deleuze, "Postscript", Negotiations, 181.

91 Marazzi, Violence, 25, 33-34.

92 Marazzi, Violence, 47.

93 Ivor Southwood, Non-Stop Inertia (Winchester, UK; Washington, USA: Zero Books, 2011), 11.

94 David Graeber, "The Debt is Not Nearly as Scary as You Think", 21st April 2011, New York Daily News. See also Harvey, Brief History of Neoliberalism, 1-2.

95 Shaviro, "'Bitter Necessity' of Debt", 8.

96 Shaviro, "'Bitter Necessity'", 9.

97 Marazzi, Violence, 94-95.

98 Sean O'Connell, Credit and Community: Working-Class Debt in the UK Since 1880 (New York: Oxford University Press, 2009), 50-52, 90, 127.

99 O'Connell, Credit and Community, 188-191.

100 Graeber, Debt: The First 5,000 Years (New York: Melville House, 2011), 361, 364, 372. On the cultural expense of the military, see Peter Sloterdijk, Critique of Cynical Reason, trans. Michael Eldred (Minneapolis: University of Minnesota Press, 2001), 323.

101 Graeber, Debt, 375-376.

102 Pasquinelli, Animal Spirits, 168.

103 O'Connell, Credit and Community, 6, 91.

104 Sarah Morrison and Brian Brady "Student debt will soar to £200bn, official figures show", Independent on Sunday, 21 August 2011.

105 Castells, Rise of the Network Society, xix.

106 Marx frequently refers to zombies, vampires and the supernatural – see Karl Marx, Capital. A Critique of Political Economy. Vol. 1. (trans. Ben Fowkes. London: Penguin, 1990), 163, 176, 189, 255, 342, 416, 502-503, 548.

107 On 'zombie banks' see Tyler Cowen, "Euro vs. Invasion of the Zombie Banks", New York Times, April 17 2011.

108 Every 'outside' is now within and 'inside' capitalist accumulation – even bankruptcy functions inside accumulation, leading to an infinite regression of debt. See Marazzi, Violence, 109-111.

109 Harvey, Condition of Postmodernity, 10-11, 16-18; Charles Baudelaire, The Painter of Modern Life and Other Essays, ed. and trans. Jonathon Mayne (London: Phaidon, 2003), 12.

110 Harvey, Condition, 240; Jameson, Postmodernism, 9-10, 16; Paul Virilio, The Information Bomb, trans. Chris Turner (London: Verso, 2005), 72, 94.

111 See Castells, Rise of the Network Society, 403-406; Gilles

Deleuze and Félix Guattari, Anti-Oedipus. Capitalism and Schizophrenia, trans. Robert Hurley, Mark Seem and Helen R. Lane (Minneapolis: University of Minnesota Press, 2000), 129-130, 134, 249-255. On the universality of digital media: Galloway and Thacker, The Exploit, 10.

112 Walter Benjamin, "The Work of Art in the Age of Mechanical Reproduction", Illuminations, ed. Hannah Arendt, trans. Harry Zorn (London: Pimlico, 1999), 215-217; Castells, Rise of the Network Society, 400-406, 508-509.

113 Berardi, Soul at Work, 21-22, 87, 131, 198; Precarious Rhapsody, 34-35; Virilio, Information Bomb, 61-65.

114 Castells, Rise of the Network Society, xxv-xxvi, 44-45, 495; Overall 27% of adults own smartphones, with 37% admitting addiction. See Ofcom, Communications Market Report: UK. 4 August 2011, 3-5.

115 Virilio, Information Bomb, 13, 94; Berardi, Soul at Work, 87-88.

116 Castells, Rise of the Network Society, xl, 495-499.

117 Castells, Rise, xx, xl-xliii, 470-481.

118 Rullani cit. in Pasquinelli, Animal Spirits, 98.

119 Richard Sennett, The Fall of Public Man (Cambridge: Cambridge University Press, 1977), 14.

120 Sennett, Fall of Public Man, 15.

121 Virilio, "The Overexposed City", from L'espace Critique (Paris: Christian Bourgeois, 1984), trans. Astrid Hustvedt for Zone 1-2 (New York: Urzone, 1986), 543. Jean Baudrillard similarly describes a transition from the Mirror Phase to the Video Phase – see Baudrillard, America, trans. Chris Turner (London: Verso, 1999), 36.

122 Berners-Lee cit. in Alexander R. Galloway, Protocol: How Control Exists After Decentralization (Cambridge, MA: MIT Press, 2004), 60 n16.

123 See also Galloway and Thacker, Exploit, 4, 30, 36, 40, 57, 60.

124 Galloway and Thacker, Exploit, 14-15.

125 Italicised in original. Galloway and Thacker, Exploit, 74.

126 On its reception see Bradley Lewis, Moving Beyond Prozac, DSM, and the New Psychiatry. The Birth of Postpsychiatry (Ann Arbor: University of Michigan Press, 2006), 2-3.

127 American Psychiatric Association, The Diagnostic and Statistical Manual of Mental Disorders IV. Text Revision. DSM-IV-TR (Arlington: American Psychiatric Association, 2004), 472.

128 In Carl Walker, Depression and Globalization: The Politics of Mental Health in the Twenty-First Century (New York: Springer, 2008), 8; NHS Information Centre, Adult Psychiatric Morbidity in England, 2007. Results of a Household Survey. (Leeds: NHS Information Centre, 2009), 11.

129 Walker, Depression and Globalization, 8; see also Catherine Sullivan on relation to depression and gender in Melancholia: Essays on Clinical Depression (London: Lightning Source, 2005), 125.

130 NHS Information Centre, Adult Psychiatric Morbidity, 27.

131 NHS Information Centre, Adult Psychiatric Morbidity, 13; Walker, Depression and Globalization, 150, 152.

132 Male unemployment has fallen 0.3 points during the same period: See Polly Curtis, "TUC warns of rise in women's job losses", The Guardian, 9 March 2011; High Pay Commission, "Director's Pensions: in it for themselves?", 11.

133 See as indicative James Groves, "David Cameron warns feckless parents who expect to raise children on benefits", Daily Mail, 14 June 2011.

134 The Fawcett Society have campaigned in the UK since 1866 to close the gender inequality gap: see their "Cutting Women Out" campaign, which identifies that women face a triple jeopardy of low pay, precarity and discrimination during times of 'austerity'. www.fawcettsociety.org.uk/index.asp?PageID=1208 [URL accessed 04/02/12].

135 NHS Information Centre, Adult Psychiatric Morbidity, 136.

136 I refer specifically to Hall's 1973 essay "Encoding, Decoding" with its polite celebration of negotiated and oppositional readings; Adorno's brutally pessimistic account of human brainwashing via the cultural industry can be found in his misanthropic "The Schema of Mass Culture" essay.

137 Walker, Depression and Globalization, 21-22; on the £20mn figure, see statistics posted by NHS London on http://data.gov.uk/dataset/london-nhs-primary-care-spend-antidepressant-drugs [URL accessed 31/03/12]; on the flurry of news coverage in April, see as indicative Staff and Press Association, "Dramatic rise in antidepressant prescriptions linked to money worries", Guardian.co.uk, 7 April 2011 www.guardian.co.uk/society/2011/apr/07/dramatic-rise-antidpressant-prescriptions-money-worries [URL accessed 31/03/12].

138 Found by the Environment Agency; Mark Townsend, "Stay calm everyone, there's Prozac in the drinking water", The Observer, 8 August 2004.

139 See Walker, Depression and Globalization, vii.

140 Figure based on earlier survey by Weich and Lewis in 1998 – see Lewis, Depression and Globalization, 138.

141 Foucault, Discipline and Punish, 138-139; Deleuze, "Postscript", Negotiations, 178.

142 See Walker, Depression and Globalization, 89, 135, 144-145, 148.

143 David Healy, The Creation of Psychopharmacology (Cambridge: Harvard University Press, 2002), 155, 215, 249.

144 On the history of psychopharmacology, see Healy, Creation of Psychopharmacology, chapters 6, 7 and 8.

145 Graeber, Debt: First 5,000 Years, 373-376.

146 Benjamin Franklin, Autobiography and Other Writings, ed. Ormond Seavey (Oxford: Oxford University Press, 1998),

266. Original italicisation removed.

147 On this see Lars Svendsen's excellent Work (Durham: Acumen, 2009), 59.

148 On the ominous fear of machinery replacing the worker and plunging her or him into abject poverty, a fear ultimately unfounded, see Karl Marx, Grundrisse, trans. Martin Nicolaus (London: Penguin, 1993), 704; Lars Svendsen, Work, 112-114.

149 Chartered Institute of Personnel and Development, Overview of CIPD Surveys: A Barometer of HR trends and developments in 2011, www.cipd.co.uk/NR/rdonlyres /315E45C9-B864-4F51-B8D5-1F39F0738DBE/0/ Overviewofsurveysandbarometer20115418.pdf, 17-23.

150 Jeremy Bentham, The Panopticon Writings, ed. Miran Božovič (London: Verso, 1995), 31.

151 F.W. Taylor, The Principles of Scientific Management (Sioux Falls: Nuvision publications, 2007), 24.

152 Mark Fisher, Capitalist Realism: Is There No Alternative (Ropley: Zero, 2009), 42.

153 Letwin speaking at KPMG, a private company winning contracts for NHS Commissioning following the abolition of NHS Primary Care Trusts, marking next stage of eventual privatisation of the increasingly-expensive NHS. Daniel Boffey, "Public sector workers need 'discipline and fear', says Oliver Letwin", The Guardian, 30 July 2011.

154 Jin, Joyce, Phillips and Sibieta, Poverty and Inequality in the UK: 2011. IFS Commentary C118, 29-30.

155 Jin et al., Poverty and Inequality in the UK, 1-3, 33, 37, 39, 65, 69.

156 Lewis, Moving Beyond Prozac, 134.

157 NHS Information Centre, Adult Psychiatric Morbidity, 27.

158 See Sigmund Freud, "Beyond the Pleasure Principle", in Beyond the Pleasure Principle and Other Writings, trans. John Reddick (London: Penguin, 2003), 50-51.

159 Freud, "Inhibition, Symptom, and Fear", in Beyond the Pleasure Principle, 172-177, 233-237.

160 Quoted in Heather Brooke, The Silent State (London: Windmill, 2011), 7.

161 On Bulger case, see Brendan O'Neill, "Watching You Watching Me", New Statesman, 2 October 2006.

162 See Chris Petit, "Smile, Honey, You're on Candid Camera", New Statesman, 21 May 2010.

163 The dubious 4.2 million figure comes from McCahill, Michael and Clive Norris, "CCTV in London. Working Paper No.6", Urbaneye: On the Threshold to Urban Panopticon? Analysing the Employment of CCTV in European Cities and Assessing its Social and Political Impacts, 20.

164 On unusable CCTV footage, see Andy McSmith, "The Big Question: Are CCTV cameras a waste of money in the fight against crime?, The Independent, 7 May 2008.

165 See BBC News, "England riots: what happened to the rioters in court?", 23 August 2011. www.bbc.co.uk/news/uk-14504294 [URL accessed 31/03/12].

166 On the local benefits in crime and fear reduction of CCTV, see Chris Sarno et al., "Developing a Picture of CCTV in Southwark Town Centres: Final Report", Criminal Policy Research Unit, South Bank University, August 1999.

167 Brooke, Silent State, 8-10, 16-18.

168 Brooke, Silent State, 8, 205.

169 Brooke, Silent State, 23, 60-62; Anna Minton, Ground Control: Fear and Happiness in the Twenty-First-Century City (London: Penguin, 2009), 152-155.

170 Nick Davies, Flat Earth News. An Award-winning Reporter Exposes Falsehood, Distortion and Propaganda in the Global Media (London: Chatto & Windus, 2008), 38; Ministry of Justice, Breaking the Cycle: Effective Punishment, Rehabilitation and Sentencing of Offenders,

December 2010 (London: HMSO, 2010), 7-8.

171 Hackney, Haringey and Lewisham all feature in a TUC survey of top ten unemployment blackspots, with UK youth unemployment now at 20.2%, or 949,000 of 16-24-year-olds, one of the highest rates in the EU. See Larry Clark, "Riot-hit London boroughs among worst unemployment blackspots", Guardian, 17 August 2011; Sean O'Grady, "Crisis Deepens for UK's Young", The Independent, 18 August 2011.

172 David Harvey, "From Managerialism to Entrepreneurialism: The Transformation in Urban Governance in Late Capitalism" in The Blackwell City Reader, ed. Gary Bridge and Sophie Watson (Malden: Blackwell, 2005), 456-458.

173 Josephine Berry Slater and Anthony Iles, No Room to Move: Radical Art and the Regenerate City (London: Mute, 2010), 11-14, 34-38; Owen Hatherley, A Guide to the New Ruins of Great Britain (London: Verso, 2010), 299-302.

174 Slater and Iles, No Room to Move, 52; Giorgio Agamben, The Coming Community, trans. Michael Hardt (Minneapolis: University of Minnesota Press, 2007), 1.

175 Oldfield Ford interviewed in Slater and Iles, No Room to Move, 110.

176 See on this Sennett, Fall of Public Man, 14-15; Minton, Ground Control, 171-178.

177 Virno, Grammar, 31-35, 39.

178 Virno, Grammar, 39; David Marquand, The Decline of the Public (Cambridge: Polity Press, 2004), 79-83.

179 Davies, Flat Earth News, 259-261, 268-276.

180 Benjamin, "The Work of Art", Illuminations, 234-235.

181 Galloway and Thacker, Exploit, 41.

182 Peter Oborne, The Triumph of the Political Class (London: Simon & Schuster, 2007), xiv-xvii.

183 Oborne, Triumph of the Political Class, 297-299.

184 See Oborne, Triumph of the Political Class, 100.

185 See Simon Rogers and Ami Sedghi, "David Cameron's

meetings with the media and Chequers guests: get the full list", Guardian.co.uk, 15 July 2011.

186 Oborne, Triumph of the Political Class, 80-87.

187 Tony Blair, speaking at the 1999 Labour Party Conference, in Oborne, Triumph of the Political Class, 107.

188 Castells, Rise of the Network Society, 507. See also Virilio, Information Bomb, 74.

189 Davies, Flat Earth News, 56-59.

190 They surveyed every domestic news item over a 2-week period in The Guardian, The Independent, The Times, Daily Telegraph and Daily Mail, 2207 items in total. The Times had reproduced PR and wire copy without any major alteration for over 69% of its content during this time. See Davies, Flat Earth News, 52.

191 On the Yes Men, see Galloway, Protocol, xvii, who also notes that the Yes Men were brought down via political pressure on their web-hosts Verio, in a strategy that was later used to destroy Wikileaks.

192 Deleuze, "Control and Becoming", Negotiations, 175.

193 In 53 speeches made by Tony Blair 1997-1999, 'new' appears 609 times; 'modern' appears 89 times; 'modernise' or 'modernisation' 87 times; and 'reform' 143 times – see Oborne, Triumph, 105.

194 Agamben, Coming Community, 80.

195 Helene Mulholland, Polly Curtis and agencies, "David Cameron promises to 'end state's monopoly' on public services", The Guardian, 11 July 2011.

196 David Cameron, in Mulholland et al., "David Cameron promises", The Guardian, 11 July 2011.

197 Mulholland et al., "David Cameron promises", Guardian, 11 July 2011.

198 UK Home Office, A New Approach to Fighting Crime, 2 March 2011, 10.

199 UK Home Office, A New Approach, 3.

200 Brooke, Silent State, 12, 34-35.

201 Edward L. Bernays, Propaganda (New York: Livewright, 1928), 9.

202 Kafka, The Castle, 512.

203 See G.W.F. Hegel, The Phenomenology of Spirit, trans. A.V. Miller (New York: Oxford University Press, 1977), Preface, §§28-33, §§53-56.

204 Kafka, Castle, 496-512.

205 Fisher, Capitalist Realism, 51-52.

206 Virno, Grammar, 86-87.

207 Pasquinelli, Animal Spirits, 192.

208 See Pascal Bruckner's diagnosis of a collective European malaise from a right-wing perspective, The Tyranny of Guilt: an Essay on Western Masochism, trans. Steven Rendall (Princeton: Princeton University Press, 2010), 34.

209 See Benjamin Noys, The Persistence of the Negative: A Critique of Contemporary Continental Theory (Edinburgh: Edinburgh University Press, 2010), 128.

210 Sloterdijk, Critique, 5.

211 Sloterdijk, Critique, 125-128.

212 Sloterdijk, Critique, 120, 124-125, 140-145, 192-193.

213 Sloterdijk, Critique, 194.

214 Ballard in Marianne Brace, "J G Ballard: The comforts of madness", The Independent, 15 September 2006.

215 See Heinz Politzer, Franz Kafka: Parable and Paradox. Revised, Expanded Edition (Ithaca, New York: Cornell University Press, 1966), 262.

216 Deleuze and Guattari, Kafka: Towards a Minor Literature, trans. Dana Polan (Minneapolis: University of Minnesota Press, 2003), 52; Kafka, Letter to His Father, trans. Ernst Kaiser and Eithne Wilkins (New York: Schocken, 1966), 111.

217 Fisher, Capitalist Realism, 21-22.

218 Davies, Flat Earth News, 36-38, 136; Oborne, Triumph, 298.

219 High Pay Commission, More for Less, 5-6. Boardroom pay is

estimated to have risen by 55% since 2010 whilst average wages have stagnated and in real terms fallen, due to increasing inflation.

220 High Pay Commission, More for Less, 10.

221 National Centre for Social Research, British Social Attitudes 27th Report. Summary. December 2010, 1-2; British Social Attitudes 28th Report. Summary. December 2011, 1-2.

222 The number of those with 'some confidence' in business diminished by the same amount to 55% – see High Pay Commission, More for Less, 18; European Commission, Special Eurobarometer 72.2. Attitudes of Europeans towards Corruption. November 2009 (Brussels: TNS Opinion & Social, 2009), 10-11, 16, 26, 28, 40. The UK is also one of the most pessimistic states: 77% of those surveyed believed corruption has always existed and is unavoidable.

223 Sloterdijk warns in Spenglerian terms of a growing 'Western irrationalism' – see Sloterdijk, Critique, 324.

224 Southwood, Non-Stop Inertia, 85-86; Noys, Persistence of the Negative, 128, 152-157, 168.

225 Marc Augé, Non-Places: Introduction to an Anthropology of Supermodernity, trans. John Howe (London:Verso, 1997), 79.

226 Augé, Non-Places, 77.

227 Augé, Non-Places, 79, 94.

228 Augé, Non-Places, 103.

229 J.G. Ballard, Kingdom Come (London: Harper Perennial, 2007), 146.

230 Ballard, Kingdom Come, 33.

231 See Artaud's essay "Theatre and the Plague" in Antonin Artaud, The Theatre and Its Double, trans. Victor Corti (London: Calder, 1993).

232 Whilst no entirely accurate statistics exist for web traffic data, on the Alexa Internet company's record of the "Top 500 Global Sites", one finds free sex chat and pornography websites well-represented – for instance Xvideos (57),

Xhamster (59), Livejasmin (75), Pornhub (79), Youporn (102), RedTube (114), Xxnx (125): www.alexa.com/topsites [URL last accessed 31/03/12] .

233 On theorisations of affective labour see Hardt and Negri, Empire, 293-295; Arlie Russell Hochschild, The Managed Heart. Commercialization of Human Feeling (Berkeley; Los Angeles: University of California Press, 2003), 7.

234 See Laurie Penny, Meat Market: Female Flesh Under Capitalism (Alresford: Zero, 2011), 16.

235 Ballard, Kingdom Come, 103.

236 'Long live the new flesh!' is also the final words of David Cronenberg's 1983 film Videodrome, which informs much of the background ideas of Chapter Eight.

237 Deleuze, Francis Bacon: The Logic of Sensation, trans. Daniel W. Smith (London: Continuum, 2004), 21.

238 Fyodor Dostoyevsky, Notes from Underground and The Double, trans. Jessie Coulson (London: Penguin, 2003), 43.

239 Ballard's phrase, in Interview, 30 Oct. 1982, in Re/Search 8/9.

240 A recent Gallup-Healthways Well-being Index has found that due to chronic and often work-related ill-health, British workers are losing over £21 billion of productivity. No doubt a Jamie Oliver get-fit scheme is in the pipeline. See Dan Witters and Cynthia English, "Unhealthy UK Workers' Lost Productivity Cost: 21 Billion Pounds" www.gallup.com/poll/149747/Unhealthy-Workers-Lost-Productivity-Cost-Billion-Pounds.aspx [URL last accessed 31/03/12].

241 Paul Mason, "Global unrest: how the revolution went viral", The Guardian, 3 January 2012.

242 For a polemical introduction to 'ruinporn' or as the author locates it, 'Detroitism', see John Michael Leary, "Detroitism", in Guernica Magazine January 15 2011, www.guernicamag.com/features/2281/leary_1_15_11/.

243 A more nuanced account of 'ruin porn' comes from Ian Ference's response to Leary's article above, "On 'Ruin Porn'",

Huffington Post January 31 2011, www.huffingtonpost .com/ian-ference/on-ruin-porn_b_816593.html.

244 See for instance Andrew Moore's Detroit Disassembled (2010); Yves Marchand and Romain Meffre's The Ruins of Detroit (2010); Julien Temple's BBC film Requiem for Detroit? (2010) – there are countless examples.

245 Susan Sontag, "The Imagination of Disaster", in Against Interpretation, and Other Essays (New York: Delta, 1967), 212.

246 John Keats, "Ode on a Grecian Urn", Selected Poems. Everyman's Poetry ed. Nicholas Roe (London: J.M. Dent, 1996), 65.

247 Rob Horning, "Detroit Ruin Porn", 20 January 2011, Marginal Utility blog, www.popmatters.com/pm/post/ 136101-/.

248 See Frédéric Chaubin's fascinating CCCP: Cosmic Communist Constructions Photographed (Köln: Taschen, 2011).

249 Think of Jane Jacobs' highly popular 1961 The Death and Life of Great American Cities, with its racialised discussion of 'barbarians' in the midst. More recently, see as indicative the comments by 'Geralyn' and others to an excellent response on ruin porn, BFP, "The Ruin Porn Post", on Feministe September 15 2011, www.feministe.us/ blog/archives/2011/09/15/the-ruin-porn-post/.

250 Marquis de Sade, The 120 Days of Sodom and Other Writings, ed. and trans. Austryn Wainhouse and Richard Seaver (New York: Grove Press, 1987), 362.

251 For one case of this, read the excellent critique of ruinporn by Thomas Morton, "Something, Something, Something, Detroit", Vice Magazine, 16 (8), www.vice.com/read/some thing-something-something-detroit-994-v16n8 [URL last accessed 31/03/12].

252 Michel Foucault, The Order of Things: An Archaeology of

the Human Sciences (London: Routledge, 2002), xix.

253 On how ruinporn images are often made by cropping, see Morton, "Something, Something, Something, Detroit", Vice Magazine 16(8).

254 Georg Simmel, "The Ruin", Essays on Sociology, Philosophy and Aesthetics, ed. Kurt H. Wolff (New York: Harper and Row, 1965), 261.

255 Primo Levi, The Drowned and the Saved, trans. Raymond Rosenthal (London: Abacus, 1989), 30.

256 Levi, Drowned and Saved, 63-64.

257 There are two instances: firstly, the contemptuous and anti-intellectual rejection of the Reading the Riots recommendations by Home Office Minister Theresa May, who has insisted on using the language of gangs, 'mobs' and criminality to describe the rioters instead of the obvious links to poverty and deprivation – see Theresa May, The Mail on Sunday, 18th December 2011. Secondly, the report by Chief of Constabulary Denis O'Connor recommending use of firearms against arsonists involved in rioting and for new and more robust measures of engagement against future disturbances, a difficult offence to prove: see Her Majesty's Inspectorate of Constabulary, The Rules of Engagement: A Review of the August 2011 Disorders, pub. 20 December 2011 [www.hmic.gov.uk/media/a-review-of-the-august-2011-disorders-20111220.pdf], 87-89, 109-110.

258 Levi, Drowned and Saved, 5, 13-18, 142-143.

259 Levi, Drowned and Saved, 135.

260 Levi, Drowned and Saved, 162.

261 See on this Stanley Milgram, Obedience to Authority: An Experimental View (London: Tavistock Publications, 1974), which sought to question in a similar vein to Levi if the atrocities of Nazis could occur again. The experiments at Yale University from 1961-2, first written about by Milgram in a 1963 journal article, demonstrated that test subjects

would generally obey an authority's instruction to increase punishment to lethal levels.

262 Levi, Drowned and Saved, 118.

263 Levi, Drowned and Saved, 167.

264 The High Pay Commission, Cheques With Balances: Why tackling high pay is in the national interest. Final report of the High Pay Commission (pub. 23 November 2011, http://highpaycommission.co.uk/wp-content/uploads /2011/11/HPC_final_report_WEB.pdf), 7.

265 High Pay Commission, Cheques With Balances, 8-9, 22-23.

266 High Pay Commission, Cheques With Balances, 8.

267 Michel de Montaigne, "II: 12. An apology for Raymond Sebond", The Complete Essays, trans. M.A Screech (London: Penguin, 2003), 500.

268 Pasquinelli, Animal Spirits, 26.

269 See for instance the rapturous conclusion of Michael Hardt and Antonio Negri, Multitude: War and Democracy in the Age of Empire (New York: Penguin Press, 2004), 358.

270 Baruch Spinoza, "Theological-Political Treatise", in Complete Works, trans. Samuel Shirley, ed. Michael L. Morgan (Indianapolis: Hackett, 2002), 566.

271 The character appears in Herman Melville's novella "Bartleby, the Scrivener": as mediocre figure of resistance, see Agamben, Coming Community, 37; Hardt and Negri, Empire, 203-4; Gilles Deleuze, "Bartleby; or, The Formula" in Essays Clinical and Critical, trans. Daniel W. Smith and Michael A. Greco (London: Verso, 1998), 69-74.

272 Walter Benjamin, "Critique of Violence", One-Way Street and Other Writings, trans. Edmund Jephcott and Kingsley Shorter (London: NLB, 1979), 139-154.

273 Dostoyevsky, Notes from Underground, 43; Pasquinelli, Animal Spirits, 102.

274 See Agamben, Homo Sacer, 72.

Contemporary culture has eliminated both the concept of the public and the figure of the intellectual. Former public spaces – both physical and cultural – are now either derelict or colonized by advertising. A cretinous anti-intellectualism presides, cheerled by expensively educated hacks in the pay of multinational corporations who reassure their bored readers that there is no need to rouse themselves from their interpassive stupor. The informal censorship internalized and propagated by the cultural workers of late capitalism generates a banal conformity that the propaganda chiefs of Stalinism could only ever have dreamt of imposing. Zer0 Books knows that another kind of discourse – intellectual without being academic, popular without being populist – is not only possible: it is already flourishing, in the regions beyond the striplit malls of so-called mass media and the neurotically bureaucratic halls of the academy. Zer0 is committed to the idea of publishing as a making public of the intellectual. It is convinced that in the unthinking, blandly consensual culture in which we live, critical and engaged theoretical reflection is more important than ever before.